Updates in Securities Regulation

Updates in Securities Regulation, 2019

Wendy Gerwick Couture
Professor of Law
University of Idaho College of Law

ASPEN
PUBLISHING

To contact Customer Service, e-mail customer.service@aspenpublishing.com, call 1-800-950-5259, or mail correspondence to:

Aspen Publishing
Attn: Order Department
PO Box 990
Frederick, MD 21705

Printed in the United States of America.

1 2 3 4 5 6 7 8 9 0

ISBN 978-1-5438-0895-7

About Aspen Publishing

Aspen Publishing is a leading provider of educational content and digital learning solutions to law schools in the U.S. and around the world. Aspen provides best-in-class solutions for legal education through authoritative textbooks, written by renowned authors, and breakthrough products such as Connected eBooks, Connected Quizzing, and PracticePerfect.

The Aspen Casebook Series (famously known among law faculty and students as the "red and black" casebooks) encompasses hundreds of highly regarded textbooks in more than eighty disciplines, from large enrollment courses, such as Torts and Contracts to emerging electives such as Sustainability and the Law of Policing. Study aids such as the *Examples & Explanations* and the *Emanuel Law Outlines* series, both highly popular collections, help law students master complex subject matter.

Major products, programs, and initiatives include:

- **Connected eBooks** are enhanced digital textbooks and study aids that come with a suite of online content and learning tools designed to maximize student success. Designed in collaboration with hundreds of faculty and students, the Connected eBook is a significant leap forward in the legal education learning tools available to students.

- **Connected Quizzing** is an easy-to-use formative assessment tool that tests law students' understanding and provides timely feedback to improve learning outcomes. Delivered through CasebookConnect.com, the learning platform already used by students to access their Aspen casebooks, Connected Quizzing is simple to implement and integrates seamlessly with law school course curricula.

- **PracticePerfect** is a visually engaging, interactive study aid to explain commonly encountered legal doctrines through easy-to-understand animated videos, illustrative examples, and numerous practice questions. Developed by a team of experts, PracticePerfect is the ideal study companion for today's law students.

- The **Aspen Learning Library** enables law schools to provide their students with access to the most popular study aids on the market across all of their courses. Available through an annual subscription, the online library consists of study aids in e-book, audio, and video formats with full text search, note-taking, and highlighting capabilities.

- Aspen's **Digital Bookshelf** is an institutional-level online education bookshelf, consolidating everything students and professors need to ensure success. This program ensures that every student has access to affordable course materials from day one.

- **Leading Edge** is a community centered on thinking differently about legal education and putting those thoughts into actionable strategies. At the core of the program is the Leading Edge Conference, an annual gathering of legal education thought leaders looking to pool ideas and identify promising directions of exploration.

Contents

About the Author

Wendy Gerwick Couture is a Professor of Law at the University of Idaho College of Law, where she teaches securities regulation, business associations, and white-collar crime. She would like to dedicate this book to her wonderful students, whose curiosity and enthusiasm inspire her work.

Updates in Securities Regulation, 2019

I. Introduction

Updates in Securities Regulation reviews the legislative, regulatory, and litigation developments in the dynamic area of securities regulation during the past year[1] and previews issues that will likely arise in the year ahead. Securities regulation is evolving in response to recent changes in technology, presidential administrations, Securities and Exchange Commission leadership, and composition of the Supreme Court. This *Update* provides a summary of developments across a variety of topics, from initial coin offerings to shareholder proposals; contextualizes those developments; and predicts their future impacts, drawing from commentary by practitioners, scholars, and regulators. This volume is intended for an audience of securities law scholars, practitioners, policymakers, and students.

II. Definition of "Security"

The Securities Act of 1933 ("Securities Act") and the Securities Exchange Act of 1934 ("Exchange Act") define "security" with a laundry list, including "stock," "notes," and "investment contracts."[2] Unforeseen by Congress in the 1930s, these definitions are now intersecting with blockchain technology and virtual space.

A. Blockchain-Based Currencies, Coins, and Tokens

The issue of whether blockchain-enabled cryptocurrencies and digital coins (or tokens) are "investment contracts" under the *Howey* test,[3] and thus subject to the securities laws, has continued to evolve rapidly. As a reminder, on July 25, 2017, the Securities and Exchange Commission ("SEC") issued a Report of Investigation Pursuant to Section 21(a) of the Securities Exchange Act of 1934 ("21(a) Report") analyzing the applicability of the securities laws to blockchain-enabled means of raising capital.[4] The 21(a) Report analyzed the following transaction:

---

1. *Updates in Securities Regulation* covers the period from September 1, 2017 to September 1, 2018.

2. 15 U.S.C. § 77b(a)(1); 15 U.S.C. § 78c(a)(10).

3. SEC v. W.J. Howey Co., 328 U.S. 293, 301 (1946) ("The test is whether the scheme involves an investment of money in a common enterprise with profits to come solely from the efforts of others.").

4. Report of Investigation Pursuant to Section 21(a) of the Securities Exchange Act of 1934, SEC Release No. 34-81207 (July 25, 2017).

The DAO is one example of a Decentralized Autonomous Organization, which is a term used to describe a "virtual" organization embodied in computer code and executed on a distributed ledger or blockchain. The DAO was created by Slock.it and Slock.it's co-founders, with the objective of operating as a for-profit entity that would create and hold a corpus of assets through the sale of DAO Tokens to investors, which assets would then be used to fund "projects." The holders of the DAO Tokens stood to share in the anticipated earnings from these projects as a return on their investment in DAO Tokens. In addition, DAO Token holders could monetize their investments in DAO Tokens by re-selling DAO Tokens on a number of web-based platforms ("Platforms") that supported secondary trading in the DAO Tokens.[5]

The 21(a) Report concluded that the DAO Tokens at issue were "investment contracts" under the *Howey* test.[6] As a consequence, under § 5 of the Securities Act,[7] "[t]he DAO was required to register the offer and sale of DAO Tokens, unless a valid exemption from such registration applied,"[8] and the Platforms that traded the DAO Tokens were required to "register as a national securities exchange or operate pursuant to an exemption from such registration."[9]

Since the issuance of the 21(a) Report, there has been additional debate about two topics: (1) under what circumstances digital coins (or tokens) issued pursuant to an initial coin offering ("ICO") are securities; and (2) whether trades in cryptocurrencies are securities transactions.

1.   *Initial Coin Offerings*

In an Initial Coin Offering ("ICO"), investors purchase a digital coin or token, paying for the digital asset with either currency or cryptocurrency. Often, the value raised via the ICO is used to develop the networks on which the coins or tokens will trade.

In the wake of the 21(a) Report, it is clear that ICOs similar to the DAO's offering must either be registered or exempt from registration. Indeed, the SEC has instituted a number of investigations and enforcement actions related to unregistered ICOs.[10] In addition, the unregistered offering of digital tokens has also led to some private securities litigation. For example, Ripple Labs Inc. is facing several putative class actions in which purchasers

---

5. *Id.* at 1.
6. *Id.* at 11-15.
7. 15 U.S.C. § 77e.
8. Report of Investigation Pursuant to Section 21(a) of the Securities Exchange Act of 1934, SEC Release No. 34-81207, at 16 (July 25, 2017).
9. *Id.* at 18.
10. *E.g.,* In re Munchee Inc., Order Instituting Cease-and-Desist Proceedings Pursuant to Section 8A of the Securities Act of 1933, Making Findings, and Imposing a Cease-and-Desist Order, SEC Release No. 10445 (Dec. 11, 2017).

of Ripple tokens ("XRP") allege that the tokens were securities under California law and that Ripple violated California law by failing to either register the tokens or satisfy an exemption from registration.[11]

Some proponents of ICOs argue, however, that there is a distinction between the offer or sale of "security tokens," like the DAO Tokens analyzed in the 21(a) Report, and "utility tokens." For example, in a white paper, the Simple Agreement for Future Tokens ("SAFT") Project describes utility tokens as follows:

> This category of blockchain tokens contains assets that do not purport to replace legacy financial services products. They are designed to offer intrinsic utility that powers a decentralized, distributed network that delivers to the users of the network a consumptive good or service. For example, when their networks are functional, some tokens will act as currencies, like bitcoins do. Some will act as staking or betting mechanisms, membership rights, or loan collateral. Some will simply act as cryptographic "coupons" redeemable for mundane goods and services like bags of ground coffee or boxes of razor blades.[12]

The white paper contends that the offer or sale of fully functional utility tokens may not meet the "expectation of profits" and "from the efforts of others" elements of the *Howey* test:

> First, it is more likely that purchasers have bought them to use them (since, unlike pre-functional utility tokens, they can be used immediately to satisfy imminent needs). Second, purchasers who buy them with an eye toward profit upon resale can expect those profits to be determined by a variety of market factors that predominate the efforts of the seller in updating the token's functionality.[13]

Therefore, these proponents argue that offers or sales of fully functional utility tokens may not be subject to the securities laws.

In recent public statements, however, SEC Chairman Jay Clayton has been skeptical about whether ICOs of utility tokens are beyond the scope of the securities laws, particularly if the tokens are being marketed for their potential to increase in value. In a December 11, 2017 public statement, Chairman Clayton issued the following warning:

---

11. Oconer v. Ripple Labs, Inc., Case No. 18-CIV-3332 (Cal. Superior Court, San Mateo County) (complaint filed June 27, 2018); Zakinov v. Ripple Labs Inc., Case No. 18-CIV-2845 (Cal. Superior Court, San Mateo County) (complaint filed June 5, 2018).

12. Juan Batiz-Benet, Jesse Clayburgh & Marco Santori, The SAFT Project: Toward a Compliance Token Sale Framework 3-4 (Oct. 2, 2017), at https://saftproject.com/static/SAFT-Project-Whitepaper.pdf (last visited Oct. 14, 2018).

13. *Id.* at 10.

Following the issuance of the 21(a) Report, certain market professionals have attempted to highlight utility characteristics of their proposed initial coin offerings in an effort to claim that their proposed tokens or coins are not securities. Many of these assertions appear to elevate form over substance. Merely calling a token a "utility" token or structuring it to provide some utility does not prevent the token from being a security. Tokens and offerings that incorporate features and marketing efforts that emphasize the potential for profits based on the entrepreneurial or managerial efforts of others continue to contain the hallmarks of a security under U.S. law.[14]

Chairman Clayton expanded on this warning in February 6, 2018 testimony before the Senate Committee on Banking, Housing, and Urban Affairs:

It is especially troubling when the promoters of these offerings emphasize the secondary market trading potential of these tokens, i.e., the ability to sell them on an exchange at a profit. In short, prospective purchasers are being sold on the potential for tokens to increase in value — with the ability to lock in these increases by reselling the tokens on a secondary market — or to otherwise profit from the tokens based on the efforts of others. These are key hallmarks of a security and a securities offering.[15]

On June 6, 2018, Chairman Clayton reiterated this concern in a television interview with CNBC's Bob Pisani:

Clayton: "Let me turn to what's a security. A token — a digital asset, where I give you my money and you go off and make a venture, you have some company you want to start or something you want to . . . ; and, in return for me giving you my money, you say, 'you know what, I'm going to give you a return, or you can get a return in the secondary market by selling your token to somebody'; that is a security, and we regulate that. We regulate the offering of that security, and we regulate the trading of that security. And that's our job, and we've been doing it for a long time."

Pisani: "So you're saying, classic definition of a security — you invest in a common enterprise with an expectation of profit. You're saying, 'the way you look at most ICOs — they are securities?'"

Clayton: "Correct."[16]

---

14. SEC Chairman Jay Clayton, Public Statement, Statement on Cryptocurrencies and Initial Coin Offerings (Dec. 11, 2017), at https://www.sec.gov/news/public-statement/statement-clayton-2017-12-11 (last visited Oct. 14, 2018).

15. SEC Chairman Jay Clayton, Chairman's Testimony on Virtual Currencies: The Roles of the SEC and CFTC (Feb. 6, 2018), at https://www.sec.gov/news/testimony/testimony-virtual-currencies-oversight-role-us-securities-and-exchange-commission (last visited Oct. 14, 2018).

16. Video Interview Between SEC Chairman Jay Clayton and CNBC's Bob Pisani (June 6, 2018), at https://www.cnbc.com/video/2018/06/06/sec-chairman-cryptocurrencies-like-bitcoin–not-securities.html (last visited August 24, 2018) (transcription by Wendy Couture).

The applicability of the securities laws to ICOs, especially to the offer and sale of utility tokens, is a hot topic to watch.

2. Trading in Cryptocurrencies

Cryptocurrencies operate like fiat currencies except they are not issued by a government. Cryptocurrencies may be issued via an ICO or via other mechanisms, such as "mining," and they can be used to purchase things of value or traded on digital currency exchanges.

An evolving issue is whether post-issuance trades in cryptocurrencies are securities transactions. If so, then offers or sales must be registered or exempt from registration, and trading platforms must be either registered with the SEC as a national securities exchange or exempt from registration.[17]

Whether a trade in a particular cryptocurrency is a securities transaction depends on the attributes of the cryptocurrency at issue. For example, in a June 6, 2018 television interview with CNBC's Bob Pisani, Chairman Clayton expressed the view that Bitcoin is not a security but declined to speculate about the status of other cryptocurrencies:

> Clayton: "Cryptocurrencies—these are replacements for sovereign currencies—replace the dollar, the yen, the euro with Bitcoin. That type of currency is not a security." . . .
>
> Pisani: "Let me move on. What about alt-coins? We have discussed Bitcoin, but there are other alt-coins out there—there is Ether, for example; there is Ripple. Is Ether a security?"
>
> Clayton: "So, Bob, I'm not going to comment on specific crypto-assets and whether they are a security or are not a security. But you captured the definition very well. Am I giving you my money for you to go off in a venture where I'm relying on your efforts and the efforts of your colleagues?"[18]

Similarly, in a June 14, 2018 speech, William Hinman, the Director of the SEC Division of Enforcement, expressed the view that trades in Bitcoin and Ether are probably not securities transactions because their networks are sufficiently decentralized such that "purchasers would no longer

---

17. SEC Divisions of Enforcement and Trading and Markets, Public Statement, Statement on Potentially Unlawful Online Platforms for Trading Digital Assets (March 7, 2018), at https://www.sec.gov/news/public-statement/enforcement-tm-statement-potentially-unlawful-online-platforms-trading (last visited Oct. 14, 2018).

18. Video Interview Between SEC Chairman Jay Clayton and CNBC's Bob Pisani (June 6, 2018), at https://www.cnbc.com/video/2018/06/06/sec-chairman-cryptocurrencies-like-bitcoin–not-securities.html (last visited August 24, 2018) (transcription by Wendy Couture).

reasonably expect a person or group to carry out essential managerial or entrepreneurial efforts"[19]:

> And so, when I look at Bitcoin today, I do not see a central third party whose efforts are a key determining factor in the enterprise. The network on which Bitcoin functions is operational and appears to have been decentralized for some time, perhaps from inception. Applying the disclosure regime of the federal securities laws to the offer and resale of Bitcoin would seem to add little value. And putting aside the fundraising that accompanied the creation of Ether, based on my understanding of the present state of Ether, the Ethereum network and its decentralized structure, current offers and sales of Ether are not securities transactions. And, as with Bitcoin, applying the disclosure regime of the federal securities laws to current transactions in Ether would seem to add little value. Over time, there may be other sufficiently decentralized networks and systems where regulating the tokens or coins that function on them as securities may not be required. And of course there will continue to be systems that rely on central actors whose efforts are a key to the success of the enterprise. In those cases, application of the securities laws protects the investors who purchase the tokens or coins.[20]

B. Instruments in Virtual Space

In a recent thought-provoking article, Professor Eric Chaffee considers the potential applicability of the securities laws to instruments "purchased and sold in virtual space based upon activity in that space."[21] He explains that these instruments "can exist within video games, virtual worlds, virtual reality, and augmented reality."[22] Although Professor Chaffee acknowledges that these instruments would likely satisfy the *Howey* test, he argues that they should be excluded from the securities laws under the "unless the context otherwise requires" clause:

> Based upon the intended scope of federal securities regulation, various constitutional law principles, and concerns about hindering creativity and regulatory experimentation, the virtual context requires that securities existing entirely within virtual space be excluded from the application of federal securities law. Various concerns exist regarding excluding such securities from the application of federal securities law. These concerns include whether the

---

19. William Hinman, Director, Division of Enforcement, Speech, Digital Asset Transactions: When *Howey* Met Gary (Plastic) (June 14, 2018), at https://www.sec.gov/news/speech/speech-hinman-061418 (last visited Oct. 14, 2018).

20. *Id.*

21. Eric C. Chaffee, *Securities Regulation in Virtual Space*, 74 WASH. & LEE L. REV. 1387, 1419 (2017).

22. *Id.*

application of federal securities regulation is necessary for investor protection, is required to prevent an unworkable patchwork of state regulation, and is needed to ensure that these rapidly developing and evolving virtual environments are properly regulated. Ultimately, the arguments for excluding such securities from the application of federal securities law outweigh the arguments for applying federal securities law.[23]

III.   Issuer Exemptions from Registration

No securities may be offered or sold unless they are either registered or exempt from registration.[24] This section highlights recent developments with respect to the Regulation D exemptions, the Rule 701 exemption, the Regulation A exemption, and the so-called "intrastate crowdfunding exemptions."

A.   Regulation D Exemptions

Regulation D contains the Rule 504, Rule 506(b), and Rule 506(c) exemptions from registration. A recent surprising Eleventh Circuit decision has raised a question about scope of safe harbor protection afforded by Rule 508 for insignificant deviations from a term, condition, or requirement of Regulation D.

Rule 508(a) provides that the failure to comply with a term, condition, or requirement of Rule 504 or Rule 506 will not result in the loss of the exemption for any offer of sale to a particular individual or entity if (1) the failure to comply "did not pertain to a term, condition or requirement directly intended to protect that particular individual or entity"; (2) the failure to comply "was insignificant with respect to the offering as a whole"; and (3) the issuer made a "good faith and reasonable attempt" to comply.[25]

Rule 508(b) limits the scope of the Rule 508 safe harbor:

> A transaction made in reliance on Rule 504 or 506 shall comply with all applicable terms, conditions and requirements of Regulation D. Where an exemption is established only though reliance upon paragraph (a) of this rule, the

---

23. *Id.* at 1455-56. For a response and contrary view, see Wendy Gerwick Couture, *The Risk of Regulatory Arbitrage: A Response to Securities Regulation in Virtual Space,* 74 WASH. & LEE L. REV. ONLINE 234, 238 (2018) ("I argue that, rather than excluding virtual transactions based on virtual activity from securities regulation altogether, these transactions should be subject to a new exemption from registration requirements but not from securities fraud prohibitions.").

24. 15 U.S.C. § 77e.

25. 17 C.F.R. § 230.508(a).

failure to comply shall nonetheless be actionable by the Commission under Section 20 of the Act.[26]

Commentators have traditionally interpreted Rule 508(b) to mean that, although issuers may rely on Rule 508 when defending themselves in private civil suits asserted by investors for failing to register their securities or satisfy an exemption from registration,[27] issuers may not rely on Rule 508 when defending themselves in enforcement proceedings brought by the SEC.[28] In 2017, however, the Eleventh Circuit held that a defendant could rely on the Rule 508(a) safe harbor in an SEC enforcement action for violating § 5 of the Securities Act.[29] The Eleventh Circuit interpreted Rule 508(b) as applying in enforcement actions premised on violations of Regulation D, not on § 5:

> Hence, we first look to the usage of the phrase "failure to comply" and note that it appears numerous times in Rule 508. It is used at the start of (a) in reference to the terms of Rules 504-506 and to describe the basic premise of the exemption; it appears in (a)(1) and (a)(2) referring back to its usage in (a); and it is used again in (a)(2) to specifically reference the terms of Rules 504-506. The word "comply" is also used in (a)(3), separately from the phrase "failure to comply," again in relation to Rules 504-506. "A standard principle of statutory construction provides that identical words and phrases within the same statute should normally be given the same meaning." . . . Given Rule 508(a)'s repeated reference to "failure to comply" in the context of compliance with the Rules of Regulation D for private offering exemptions, it follows that the phrase "failure to comply" in Rule 508(b) must be interpreted in the same manner: relating to compliance with Rules 504-506 of Regulation D and not to compliance with Section 5. . . .

> Second, if the SEC had intended for Rule 508(b) to address non-compliance with Section 5 of the Act, it would have expressly stated so. This is true especially because Rule 508(a), part of the same rule, explicitly references Section 5 of the Securities Act. . . .

> Third, "statutes should be construed so that no clause, sentence, or word shall be superfluous, void, or insignificant." . . . The district court's interpretation of Rule 508 runs counter to this instruction. The district court's interpretation renders the entire first sentence of Rule 508(b)—providing that "[a] transaction made in reliance on § 230.504, § 230.505, or § 230.506 shall comply with all applicable terms, conditions and requirements of Regulation

---

26. 17 C.F.R. § 230.508(b).
27. 15 U.S.C. § 77l(a)(2).
28. *E.g.*, THOMAS LEE HAZEN, 1 LAW SEC. REG. § 4:81, REGULATION D — SCOPE AND EXTENT OF REGULATION D EXEMPTIONS ("Rule 508's safe harbor for certain noncompliance with Regulation D only affects claims by private parties. Rule 508 does not preclude SEC actions in such instances.").
29. SEC v. Levin, 849 F.3d 995, 1004-05 (11th Cir. 2017).

D"—superfluous. The inclusion of this first sentence adds meaning to Rule 508(b) only if it is interpreted as allowing the SEC to bring Section 20 enforcement actions for specific violations of the rules of Regulation D, not of Section 5 of the Securities Act, even where Rule 508(a) good faith compliance applies. Otherwise, the sentence is not necessary.

In sum, the first part of the first sentence is necessary to qualify the second part of the sentence. The first sentence provides context, and the two sentences in Rule 508(b) explain that a transaction made in reliance upon the Regulation D private offering exemption generally must comply with all its terms, but if a transaction violates those terms and is saved by Rule 508's safe harbor provision, those specific violations are actionable even though the transaction is otherwise exempt.[30]

As explained by William O. Fisher, the Eleventh Circuit's analysis "makes little sense":[31]

> Section 5 contains the registration requirement. Regulation D provides one of a number of exemptions from that requirement. Choice of a Regulation D exemption is voluntary. It is not required. It is therefore odd to analyze a failure to meet a condition of one of the Regulation D exemptions as a "violation" that would be actionable by the Commission — as opposed to an action by the Commission against the issuer for violating the statute (here section 5) from which Regulation D provides an exemption.[32]

It remains to be seen, however, whether other circuits will follow the Eleventh Circuit's lead and whether the SEC will amend Rule 508(b) to clarify its meaning.[33] In the meantime, issuers defending themselves in SEC enforcement proceedings for violating § 5 by failing to satisfy a Regulation D exemption will likely seek to invoke the protection of Rule 508(a).

B.   Rule 701

Rule 701 is an exemption from registration available to non-reporting issuers for securities issued in compensatory circumstances.[34] Rule 701(e) requires issuers to provide investors with a copy of the compensatory benefit plan or contract. In addition, Rule 701(e) requires issuers to provide enhanced disclosures, including risk factors and financial statements, if

---

30. *Id.* at 1003-04.
31. *Caselaw Developments 2017*, 73 Bus. Law. 877, 892 (2018).
32. *Id.* at 892-93.
33. *Id.* at 893 ("The SEC may need to clarify 508(b), but *Levin* seems a poor interpretation of it.").
34. 17 C.F.R. § 230.701.

the aggregate sales price or amount of securities sold during any consecutive 12-month period exceeds a certain dollar amount threshold.

Since 1999, the dollar amount threshold triggering enhanced disclosure requirements has been $5 million.[35] In 2018, however, Congress enacted the Economic Growth, Regulatory Relief, and Consumer Protection Act, which directed the SEC to increase the threshold to $10 million.[36] According to the legislative history, this provision was responsive to concerns that "the disclosures make it more expensive for companies to compensate their employees with the company's stock" and that the "disclosure requirements put private companies at risk of disclosing confidential financial information."[37]

Accordingly, effective July 23, 2018, the SEC amended Rule 507(e) to require enhanced disclosures to investors only "if the aggregate sales price or amount of securities sold during any consecutive 12-month period exceeds $10 million."[38] In a client memorandum, Skadden, Arps, Slate, Meagher & Flom LLP summarized the impact of this amendment as follows:

> The ability of companies to more easily issue equity awards with greater value in lieu of cash compensation certainly is a welcome development, particularly for many early-stage companies. However, given the very modest increase in the enhanced disclosure threshold from $5 million to $10 million, we expect the impact of this rulemaking to be incremental.[39]

C.   Regulation A Exemption

The Jumpstart Our Business Startups Act ("JOBS Act") of 2012 directed the SEC to adopt new rules exempting the offering of up to $50 million of securities within a 12-month period.[40] Accordingly, effective June 19, 2015, the SEC promulgated final rules amending then-existing Regulation A to include two tiers, with Tier 1 available for offerings of up to $20 million and

---

35. Rule 701—Exempt Offerings Pursuant to Compensatory Arrangements, SEC Release No. 33-7645 (March 8, 1999).

36. Economic Growth, Regulatory Relief, and Consumer Protection Act, Pub. L. No 115-174, § 507 (May 24, 2018).

37. Report of the Financial Services Committee of the House of Representatives to H.R. 1343, at 2 (March 29, 2017).

38. Exempt Offerings Pursuant to Compensatory Arrangements, SEC Release No. 33-10520 (July 18, 2018).

39. Skadden, Arps, Slate, Meagher & Flom LLP, *SEC Eases Disclosure Threshold Under Rule 701* (July 19, 2018), at https://www.skadden.com/insights/publications/2018/07/sec-eases-disclosure-threshold-under-rule-701 (last visited September 8, 2018).

40. Jumpstart Our Business Startups Act, Pub. L. No. 112-106, § 401, 126 Stat. 306 (April 5, 2012) (codified at Section 3(b)).

Tier 2 for offerings of up to $50 million.[41] This new version of Regulation A is sometimes colloquially referred to as "Regulation A+."

Under the pre-2015 version of Regulation A, reporting companies were not eligible to rely on the exemption. When adopting the 2015 amendments to Regulation A, the SEC considered whether to expand the scope of eligible issuers to include reporting companies, but it ultimately declined to do so:

> [W]e recognize that expanding the categories of eligible issuers, as suggested by a number of commenters, could provide certain benefits, including increased investment opportunities for investors and avenues for capital formation for certain issuers. We are concerned, however, about the implications of extending issuer eligibility before the Commission has the ability to assess the impact of the changes to Regulation A being adopted today. In light of these changes, we believe it prudent to defer expanding the categories of eligible issuers (for example, by including non-Canadian foreign issuers, BDCs, or Exchange Act reporting companies) until the Commission has had the opportunity to observe the use of the amended Regulation A exemption and assess any new market practices as they develop.[42]

In 2018, however, Congress enacted the Economic Growth, Regulatory Relief, and Consumer Protection Act, which directed the SEC to amend Rule 251 of Regulation A "to remove the requirement that the issuer not be subject to section 13 or 15(d) of the Securities Exchange Act of 1934 (15 U.S.C. 78a et seq.) immediately before the offering."[43] The SEC has not yet implemented this amendment to Regulation A.

According to the legislative history, making Regulation A available to reporting companies was intended to "facilitate capital formation for small reporting companies and provide small-dollar investors with enhanced investment opportunities and facilitate liquidity in the capital markets for these smaller companies."[44] As explained in a blog post by attorneys at Sheppard Mullin, "[t]his development may be significant for smaller issuers with market capitalizations under $75 million who are subject to Exchange Act reporting requirements and whose securities trade on the over-the-counter markets, as larger, more seasoned issuers (as well as issuers who are listed on a national exchange such as NASDAQ or the NYSE) are

---

41. Amendments for Small and Additional Issues Exemptions under the Securities Act (Regulation A), SEC Release No. 33-9741 (March 25, 2015); 17 C.F.R. §§ 230.251-230.263.

42. Amendments for Small and Additional Issues Exemptions under the Securities Act (Regulation A), SEC Release No. 33-9741, at 24 (March 25, 2015).

43 Economic Growth, Regulatory Relief, and Consumer Protection Act, Public L. No. 115-174, § 508 (May 24, 2018).

44. House Report Accompanying H.R.2864 (September 5, 2017).

potentially eligible to use Form S-3 to gain quick access to capital from investors who value free-trading securities."[45]

D.   Intrastate Crowdfunding Exemptions

A relatively recent phenomenon has been the rise of "intrastate crowd-funding," which differs from nationwide crowdfunding under the federal crowdfunding exemption.[46] Under intrastate crowdfunding, an issuer must satisfy (1) a federal intrastate offering exemption and (2) a state intrastate crowdfunding exemption. In short, intrastate crowdfunding allows issuers within a state to use the Internet to sell securities to residents of that state.

Most state intrastate crowdfunding exemptions were originally tied to the federal Rule 147 intrastate offering exemption,[47] which is a safe harbor under Section 3(a)(11) of the Securities Act.[48] However, Rule 147 is an imperfect tool to accomplish intrastate crowdfunding because (1) the requirement that "offers" be made only to in-state residents[49] is difficult to satisfy when using the Internet;[50] and (2) the in-state residency test for issuers (which requires that the entity have its principal place of business in the state *and* be organized or incorporated in the state[51]) cannot be satisfied if the entity is organized or incorporated in another state (*e.g.*, Delaware).

Therefore, effective April 20, 2017, under its general exemptive authority,[52] the SEC promulgated a new federal intrastate offering exemption, Rule 147A,[53] in order to "facilitate capital formation, including through offerings relying upon intrastate crowdfunding provisions under state law, while maintaining appropriate investor protections and providing state securities regulators with the flexibility to add additional investor protections they deem appropriate for offerings within their state."[54] Rule 147A

---

45. Alexander Yarbrough, Jeffrey Fessler & Robert Wernli, Jr., *New Law Requires SEC to Expand Regulation A+ to Exchange Act Reporting Companies*, CORPORATE & SECURITIES LAW BLOG (June 19, 2018), at https://www.corporatesecuritieslawblog.com/2018/06/expand-regulation-a-exchange-act/ (last visited September 8, 2018).

46. 17 C.F.R. §§ 227.100-227.503.

47. 17 C.F.R. § 230.147.

48. 15 U.S.C. § 77c(a)(11).

49. 17 C.F.R. § 230.147(d).

50. *See* Exemptions to Facilitate Intrastate and Regional Securities Offerings, SEC Release No. 33-10238, at 17 (Oct. 26, 2016) ("The Internet, however, is not similarly targeted to residents of a particular state, making it difficult for issuers to keep the distribution of such offers local in nature.").

51. 17 C.F.R. § 230.147(c)(1)(i).

52. 15 U.S.C. § 77z-3.

53. 17 C.F.R. § 230.147A.

54. Exemptions to Facilitate Intrastate and Regional Securities Offerings, SEC Release No. 33-10238, at 1 (Oct. 26, 2016).

requires all "sales" to be made to in-state residents, but it does not require "offers" to be limited to in-state residents.[55] In addition, Rule 147A's in-state residency test for issuers requires the entity to have its principal place of business in the state, but it does not require the entity to be organized or incorporated in the state.[56]

In the wake of Rule 147A's adoption, states have begun amending their intrastate crowdfunding exemptions to allow issuers to rely on Rule 147A. For example, effective October 30, 2017, Michigan's intrastate crowdfunding exemption now permits issuers to rely on either Rule 147 or Rule 147A.[57] This trend will likely continue.[58]

IV.   Public Offerings and Trading

The public securities markets enable issuers to access vast amounts of capital and investors to trade across impersonal platforms. In the past year, there have been significant developments seeking to ease issuers' access to capital markets and to regulate algorithmic and high frequency trading.

A.   Public Offerings

According to a recent report by the Department of Treasury, "over the last two decades, the number of domestic public companies listed in the United States has declined by nearly 50%."[59] Against that backdrop, the SEC has recently implemented several reforms that seek to make access to the public markets less expensive by broadening the definition of "smaller reporting company" and expanding the availability of confidential review of registration statements. In addition, SEC Chairman Jay Clayton has previewed the potential for forthcoming proposals to raise the thresholds that trigger § 404(b) of the Sarbanes-Oxley Act and to expand the availability of "test the waters" provisions beyond emerging growth companies.

55. 17 C.F.R. § 230.147A(d).
56. 17 C.F.R. § 230.147A(c)(1).
57. Mich. Comp. Laws Ann. § 451.2202a (West) (as amended by P.A.2017, No. 141, effective Oct. 30, 2017).
58. *See* North American Securities Administrators Association, Intrastate Crowdfunding Resource Center, at http://www.nasaa.org/industry-resources/corporation-finance/instrastate-crowdfunding-resource-center/ (last visited Sept. 8, 2018) (providing a directory of the status of intrastate crowdfunding in each state).
59. U.S. Department of the Treasury, A Financial System That Creates Economic Opportunities: Capital Markets, at 21 (Oct. 2017), at https://www.treasury.gov/press-center/press-releases/Documents/A-Financial-System-Capital-Markets-FINAL-FINAL.pdf (last visited Oct. 14, 2018).

1. Smaller Reporting Companies

On June 28, 2018, the SEC adopted amendments to the definition of "smaller reporting company" ("SRC") in order to "expand the number of registrants that qualify" and thereby "reduce compliance costs for these registrants and promote capital formation, while maintaining appropriate investor protections."[60] Issuers that qualify as SRCs are subject to scaled disclosure requirements under Regulations S-K and S-X.[61]

Before the amendment, an issuer qualified as a SRC if it satisfied one of two tests: (1) public float of less than $75 million; or (2) less than $50 million of annual revenues and no public float.[62] As amended, an issuer qualifies as a SRC if it satisfies one of two tests: (1) public float of less than $250 million; or (2) less than $100 million of annual revenues and either (a) no public float or (b) public float of less than $700 million.[63]

Most striking under the amended test, an issuer with a public float of up to $700 million can qualify as a SRC if its annual revenues are less than $100 million. The SEC explained this decision, which was not included in the proposed rule, as follows:

> We are persuaded by commenters' suggestions that it is appropriate to provide a measure by which a registrant with a public float but limited revenues may qualify as a SRC. This amended revenue test expands the proposed revenue threshold for companies with no public float to permit registrants with a public float that is less than $700 million to qualify based on their revenues. . . . This change from the proposal permits some additional registrants to qualify as SRCs, and we believe that these low-revenue registrants would benefit from the cost savings of scaled disclosure accommodations and could redirect those savings into growing their businesses without significantly detracting from investor protections. For example, these registrants will remain liable for their disclosures, will continue to be required to provide all material information necessary to make any required statements not misleading, and will continue to be subject to the Division of Corporation Finance's filing review process.
>
> The amended revenue test that we are adopting is consistent with the position expressed by several commenters that it is not necessary to subject capital-intensive, low-revenue registrants with larger public floats or market capitalizations to the same reporting requirements as registrants with larger public floats and more well-established, revenue-generating businesses.[64]

---

60. Amendments to Smaller Reporting Co. Definition, SEC Release No. 33-10513, at 1 (June 28, 2018).
61. *Id.* at 7-9 (summarizing these scaled disclosure obligations in a chart).
62. *Id.* at 11.
63. *Id.*
64. *Id.* at 20-21.

2.   Confidential Review

Effective July 10, 2017, all companies can submit draft registration statements related to initial public offerings for confidential review by the SEC, similar to the benefit that the JOBS Act affords to emerging growth companies.[65] As explained by commentators, "[t]he confidential submission process is intended to give issuers more flexibility to plan their offerings and reduce the potential for lengthy exposure to market fluctuations that can adversely affect an offering."[66] In addition, as hypothesized by Professor Usha Rodrigues, confidential review has the potential to lower underwriting spreads:

> If the SEC has serious reservations about the issuer's early disclosures, the underwriter can learn about those reservations and address them before embarking on the offering. Alternatively, the underwriter can decide that the issuer is not a good candidate for underwriting at all, thus saving the expense of further drafting, due diligence, and a road show for an offering destined to falter or fail. To the extent that the 7% discount includes an extra allowance to account for the possibility of ultimate failure, underwriters can reduce this allowance. . . . The comfort that SEC review provides should result in fewer ultimately aborted offerings progressing farther than they ought to. Road shows are expensive; to reach an ideal level of subscriptions, the underwriter and issuer devote considerable resources, including human capital, toward reaching and enticing investors. Thus, if confidential filings help underwriters diagnose problems early then they can help underwriters pull doomed offerings before road show and other sales expenses are incurred. Moreover, if many of these underwriting costs decline, there is less need for underwriters to cover the cost of failed offerings, so that we should expect the ultimate underwriting discount to decrease accordingly. In short, in a competitive market we would expect to see a reduction in gross spreads.[67]

3.   Potential Increase in Section 404(b) Thresholds

Currently, pursuant to § 404(b) of the Sarbanes-Oxley Act[68] as amended by § 989G of the Dodd-Frank Act,[69] companies with a public float of at

65. SEC, Announcement, Draft Registration Statement Processing Procedures Expanded (June 29, 2017) (supplemented Aug. 17, 2017), at https://www.sec.gov/corpfin/announcement/draft-registration-statement-processing-procedures-expanded (last visited Oct. 14, 2017).

66. Paul Weiss Capital Markets & Securities (July 7, 2017), at https://www.paulweiss.com/practices/transactional/capital-markets-securities/publications/sec-permits-all-issuers-to-submit-certain-registration-statements-on-a-confidential-basis?id=24514 (last visited Oct. 14, 2018).

67. Usha Rodrigues, *The Effect of the Jobs Act on Underwriting Spreads*, 102 Ky. L.J. 925, 931-32 (2014).

68. Sarbanes-Oxley Act of 2002, Pub. L. No. 107-204, § 404(b), 116 Stat 745 (July 30, 2002).

69. Dodd-Frank Wall Street Reform and Consumer Protection Act, Pub. L. No. 111-203, § 989G, 124 Stat 1376 (July 21, 2010) ("Subsection (b) shall not apply with respect to any audit report prepared for an issuer that is neither a 'large accelerated filer' nor an 'accelerated filer' as those terms are defined in Rule 12b-2 of the Commission.").

least $75 million are required to include in their annual reports filed with the SEC an auditor attestation report on internal control over financial reporting. In a recent speech, SEC Chairman Jay Clayton suggested that the SEC might consider raising the thresholds that trigger § 404(b):

> Despite all of the recent efforts at the SEC, I believe more must be done to encourage capital formation for emerging companies seeking to enter our public capital markets. Over the next several months I expect the Commission will be taking a fresh look at the thresholds that trigger Section 404(b) of the Sarbanes-Oxley Act of 2002, which requires certain registrants to provide an auditor attestation report on internal control over financial reporting ("ICFR").

> While Section 404(b) is an important component of our public company regulatory regime, we have heard from market participants and our former Advisory Committee for Small and Emerging Companies that, particularly for smaller companies, the costs associated with this requirement can divert significant capital from the core business needs of companies without meaningful benefit.

> . . .

> I also believe there may be other categories of small and emerging companies where a scaled approach may be appropriate. For example, for a biotech company with routine financial statements and no revenue, the money that goes to pay for the Section 404(b) auditor attestation report could instead be used to hire new scientists to advance life-enhancing or life-saving developments. I have directed Commission staff to formulate recommendations for possible amendments that would reduce the number of companies that need to provide the auditor attestation report required by Section 404(b) while maintaining appropriate investor protections, and they are actively working on that project. I look forward to considering the staff's recommendations.[70]

4.   Potential Expansion of Ability to "Test the Waters"

Generally, companies are prohibited from communicating with potential investors about an offering before a registration statement is filed, lest they run afoul of the prohibition on "gun-jumping" during the pre-filing period.[71] Under the JOBS Act, however, emerging growth companies are permitted to communicate with qualified institutional buyers and institutional accredited investors before filing a registration statement in order to

---

70. SEC Chairman Jay Clayton, Remarks on Capital Formation at the Nashville 36/86 Entrepreneurship Festival (Aug. 29, 2018), at https://www.sec.gov/news/speech/speech-clayton-082918 (last visited Oct. 14, 2018).

71. 15 U.S.C. § 77e.

"test the waters."[72] In a recent speech, SEC Chairman Jay Clayton previewed the possibility of expanding the ability to "test the waters" to other issuers:

> [T]he staff is working on a recommendation to expand the ability of companies who are contemplating raising capital to "test the waters." The JOBS Act permitted emerging growth companies to test the waters, that is engage in communications with certain potential investors prior to or following the filing of a registration statement for an IPO. I have seen firsthand how this has benefitted companies considering an IPO, as they are able to engage investors earlier to explain their business and obtain feedback in advance of an offering. This also benefits investors and shareholders as companies are better able to determine the appropriate time for an offering and to more effectively size and price the offering. I look forward to the Commission considering this initiative in the coming year.[73]

B.   Algorithmic and High Frequency Trading

Under algorithmic trading, computers "make independent trading decisions."[74] Professor Chris Brummer explains this process as follows:

> Computer decisions are based on algorithms—set procedures and functions—to program trading in such a way as to respond to new data according to the pre-set objectives or functions of investors. These algorithms are designed to deliver the highest return, or risk-adjusted return, and define certain kinds of parameters to be included in the risk calculation. For example, market liquidity, volatility, or other factors could be introduced into the basic trade execution programming, and through these analytic variables, an automated trade decision is made.

> By creating programs to respond instantaneously to new information, algorithmic trading enables degrees of data analysis and execution speed previously unattainable. Early on, traders would be able to simultaneously analyze and compare the movements of not just three stocks or thirty, but thousands, at a time, every second. And with time, traders developed ever more complex execution models that attempted to maximize the objective function established by programmers in more novel and advanced ways. Programs not only calculate trades, and execute them in increasingly elaborate manners, but

---

72. Jumpstart Our Business Startups Act, Pub. L. No. 112-106, § 105(d), 126 Stat. 306 (April 5, 2012).

73. SEC Chairman Jay Clayton, Remarks on Capital Formation at the Nashville 36/86 Entrepreneurship Festival (Aug. 29, 2018), at https://www.sec.gov/news/speech/speech-clayton-082918 (last visited Oct. 14, 2018).

74. Chris Brummer, *Disruptive Technology and Securities Regulation*, 84 FORDHAM L. REV. 977, 1001 (2015).

also sift through data variables to identify the most relevant inputs and to learn from the evolving movements or actions of other market participants.[75]

Professor Charles R. Korsmo further explains that high-frequency trading ("HFT"), which is "characterized by very rapid trading at an extremely high volume," is a subset of algorithmic trading: "While algorithmic trading is nothing new—particularly algorithmic execution of orders involving human judgment—what is new is the rapid, computerized placement of orders that removes the human element from the decision-making process altogether."[76]

Although algorithmic and HFT trading have myriad potential benefits,[77] they also pose risks. Perhaps most famous is the so-called "Flash Crash" of May 6, 2010.[78] In a joint report about the events of May 6, the staffs of the Commodity Futures Trading Commission and the SEC identified several key lessons, including the following:

> One key lesson is that under stressed market conditions, the automated execution of a large sell order can trigger extreme price movements, especially if the automated execution algorithm does not take prices into account. Moreover, the interaction between automated execution programs and algorithmic trading strategies can quickly erode liquidity and result in disorderly markets.[79]

As one response,[80] the SEC approved a pilot "Plan to Address Extraordinary Market Volatility,"[81] submitted by the national securities exchanges and the Financial Industry Regulatory Authority ("FINRA") pursuant to Rule 608 of Regulation NMS,[82] which seeks to address these risks by implementing a "'limit up-limit down' mechanism that prevents

---

75. *Id.* at 1001-02.

76. Charles R. Korsmo, *High-Frequency Trading: A Regulatory Strategy*, 48 U. RICH. L. REV. 523, 539-40 (2014).

77. *See id.* at 549-50.

78. Consolidated Audit Trail, SEC Release No. 34-67457 (July 18, 2012) ("[O]n the afternoon of May 6, 2010, the U.S. equity and equity futures markets experienced a sudden breakdown of orderly trading, when broad-based indices, such as the Dow Jones Industrial Average Index and the S&P 500 Index, fell about 5% in just five minutes, only to rebound soon after (the "Flash Crash"). Many individual equities suffered even worse declines, with prices in over 300 stocks and exchange-traded funds falling more than 60%. In many of these cases, trades were executed at a penny or less in stocks that were trading at prices of $30 or more only moments earlier before prices recovered to their pre-Flash Crash levels.").

79. Report of the Staffs of the CFTC and SEC to the Joint Advisory Committee on Emerging Regulatory Issues, Findings Regarding the Market Events of May 6, 2010 (Sept. 30, 2010), at https://www.sec.gov/news/studies/2010/marketevents-report.pdf (last visited Sept. 9, 2018).

80. For an overview of regulatory responses, see Charles R. Korsmo, *High-Frequency Trading: A Regulatory Strategy*, 48 U. RICH. L. REV. 523, 580-87 (2014).

81. SEC Release No. 34-67091 (May 31, 2012). A current version of the Plan, as amended seventeen times, is available here: http://www.luldplan.com/plans.html (last visited Sept. 9, 2018).

82. 17 C.F.R. § 242.608.

trades in individual exchange-listed stocks from occurring outside of a specified price band."[83] The SEC recently approved an extension of the pilot period for this Plan, as amended, to April 15, 2019 and "reiterate[d] its expectation that the Participants will continue to monitor the scope and operation of the Plan and study the data produced, and will propose any modifications to the Plan that may be necessary or appropriate."[84]

As another response, the SEC adopted Rule 613 of Regulation NMS, which requires the national securities exchanges and FINRA to jointly file "a national market system plan to govern the creation, implementation, and maintenance of a consolidated audit trail and central repository."[85] The SEC summarized the benefits of a consolidated audit trail (or "CAT") as follows:

> The Commission believes that the Rule adopted today is an appropriate step in the creation of a consolidated audit trail which, when implemented, should substantially enhance the ability of the SROs and the Commission to oversee today's securities markets and fulfill their responsibilities under the federal securities laws. Rule 613 requires the submission of an NMS plan to create, implement, and maintain the first comprehensive audit trail for the U.S. securities markets, which will allow for the prompt and accurate recording of material information about all orders in NMS securities, including the identity of customers, as these orders are generated and then routed throughout the U.S. markets until execution, cancellation, or modification. This information will be consolidated and made readily available to regulators in a uniform electronic format.[86]

The implementation of the CAT plan has been significantly delayed. In recent Congressional testimony, SEC Chairman Jay Clayton explained the delay as follows:

> Under the CAT NMS Plan, the self-regulatory organizations (SROs) — the national securities exchanges and FINRA — are responsible for developing and implementing the CAT and were required to begin reporting data to the CAT by November 15, 2017. The SROs missed that deadline, and they remain out of compliance with the CAT NMS Plan today. Progress is being made. But the process remains slow and cumbersome, due largely to what I believe are issues relating to governance and project management by the SROs. We are actively encouraging the SROs to set forth a timeline of detailed, objective

---

83. SEC, Press Release, SEC Approves Proposals to Address Extraordinary Volatility in Individual Stocks and Broader Stock Market (June 1, 2012), at https://www.sec.gov/news/press-release/2012-2012-107htm (last visited Sept. 9, 2018).

84. Joint Industry Plan; Order Approving the Seventeenth Amendment to the National Market System Plan to Address Extraordinary Volatility, SEC Release No. 34-83044 (April 12, 2018).

85. 17 C.F.R. § 242.613(a)(1).

86. Consolidated Audit Trail, SEC Release No. 34-67457 (July 18, 2012).

and achievable milestones, clearly defined progress objectives for the SROs and Thesys (the plan processor) and a comprehensive description of the functionality that will be developed by specified dates.[87]

A summary of the revised proposed CAT plan timetable is available on the SEC website.[88]

Congress is also concerned about the risks associated with algorithmic trading. The Economic Growth, Regulatory Relief, and Consumer Protection Act of 2018 directs the SEC to, within 18 months, submit a report to Congress on "the risks and benefits of algorithmic trading in capital markets in the United States."[89] In particular, the report must include the following:

(1) An assessment of the effect of algorithmic trading in equity and debt markets in the United States on the provision of liquidity in stressed and normal market conditions.

(2) An assessment of the benefits and risks to equity and debt markets in the United States by algorithmic trading.

(3) An analysis of whether the activity of algorithmic trading and entities that engage in algorithmic trading are subject to appropriate Federal supervision and regulation.

(4) A recommendation of whether—

(A) based on the analysis described in paragraphs (1), (2), and (3), any changes should be made to regulations; and

(B) the Securities and Exchange Commission needs additional legal authorities or resources to effect the changes described in subparagraph (A).

V. *Mandatory Disclosures in SEC Filings*

Reporting companies are required to make extensive disclosures in periodic SEC filings. In the past year, the SEC has made progress in its ongoing review of disclosure effectiveness; quarterly financial reporting has become a hot topic; the SEC has issued guidance on pay ratio disclosure; Congress

---

87. Testimony by SEC Chairman Jay Clayton, "Oversight of the U.S. Securities and Exchange Commission," House Committee on Financial Services (June 21, 2018), at https://www.sec.gov/news/testimony/testimony-oversight-us-securities-and-exchange-commission#_ftnref4 (last visited Sept. 9, 2018).

88. Public Statement by Brett Redfearn, Director, SEC Division of Trading and Markets, Statement on Status of the Consolidated Audit Trail (Aug. 27, 2018), at https://www.sec.gov/news/public-statement/tm-status-consolidated-audit-trail#_ftn3 (last visited Sept. 9, 2018).

89. Economic Growth, Regulatory Relief, and Consumer Protection Act, Pub. L. No. 115-174, § 502 (May 24, 2018).

has again stymied political spending disclosure; and scholars have petitioned the SEC for rulemaking on environmental, social, and governance disclosure.

A. Disclosure Effectiveness Review—Regulations S-K and S-X

The SEC is engaged in an ongoing review of disclosure effectiveness, whereby the staff is considering ways to improve the disclosure requirements in Regulations S-K and S-X:

> The goal is to comprehensively review the requirements and make recommendations on how to update them to facilitate timely, material disclosure by companies and shareholders' access to that information. Initially, the review will focus on the business and financial disclosures required by periodic and current reports, Forms 10-K, 10-Q, and 8-K. Subsequent phases of the project will include compensation and governance information included in proxy statements.[90]

This disclosure effectiveness review overlaps with two directives from Congress. First, in 2012, the JOBS Act required the SEC to conduct a review of Regulation S-K to "(1) comprehensively analyze the current registration requirements of such regulation; and (2) determine how such requirements can be updated to modernize and simplify the registration process and reduce the costs and other burdens associated with these requirements for issuers who are emerging growth companies."[91] The JOBS Act also required the SEC to submit a report of the review to Congress, including "specific recommendations of the Commission on how to streamline the registration process in order to make it more efficient and less burdensome for the Commission and for prospective issuers who are emerging growth companies."[92]

Second, in 2015, the Fixing America's Surface Transportation Act (the "FAST Act") directed the SEC to modernize and simplify the requirements in Regulation S-K in order to "further scale or eliminate requirements of regulation S-K, in order to reduce the burden on emerging growth companies, accelerated filers, smaller reporting companies, and other smaller issuers, while still providing all material information to investors" and to

---

90. SEC, Disclosure Effectiveness, at https://www.sec.gov/spotlight/disclosure-effectiveness.shtml (last visited Sept. 9, 2018).

91. Jumpstart Our Business Startups Act, Pub. L. No. 112-106, § 108, 126 Stat. 306 (April 5, 2012).

92. *Id.*

"eliminate provisions of regulation S-K, required for all issuers, that are duplicative, overlapping, outdated, or unnecessary."[93] The FAST Act also directed the SEC to conduct a study on modernizing and simplifying Regulation S-K and to submit a report to Congress containing findings and detailed recommendations.[94]

In the process of this disclosure review, the SEC has published two reports about potential improvements to Regulations S-K and S-X: (1) SEC Staff, Report on Review of Disclosure Requirements in Regulation S-K as Required by Section 108 of the Jumpstart Our Business Startups Act (Dec. 2013);[95] and (2) SEC Staff, Report on Modernization and Simplification of Regulation S-K as Required by Section 72003 of the Fixing America's Surface Transportation Act (Nov. 23, 2016).[96] The SEC has also sought public comment on the effectiveness of various aspects of Regulations S-K and S-X: (1) Concept Release on Business and Financial Disclosure Required by Regulation S-K (Apr. 13, 2016);[97] and (2) Request for Comment on the Effectiveness of Financial Disclosures About Entities Other Than The Registrant (Sept. 25, 2015).[98]

The disclosure effectiveness review has already resulted in some rule-making. On August 17, 2018, the SEC approved a final rule, in a release titled "Disclosure Update and Simplification," which amends certain disclosure requirements "that have become redundant, duplicative, overlapping, outdated, or superseded, in light of other Commission disclosure requirements, U.S. Generally Accepted Accounting Principles ('U.S. GAAP'), or changes in the information environment."[99] For example, the final rules remove the requirement in Item 101(b) of Regulation S-K to provide financial information about segments in the business description section because this information is available in the notes to the financial statements.[100] Of note, the SEC declined to remove the legal proceedings disclosures required by Item 103 of Regulation S-K. Despite significant overlap with the loss contingency disclosures required by GAAP, these disclosure

---

93. FAST Act, Pub. L. No. 114-94, § 72002 (Dec. 4, 2015).

94. FAST Act, Pub. L. No. 114-94, § 72003 (Dec. 4, 2015).

95. SEC Staff, Report on Review of Disclosure Requirements in Regulation S-K As Required by Section 108 of the Jumpstart Our Business Startups Act (Dec. 2013), at https://www.sec.gov/news/studies/2013/reg-sk-disclosure-requirements-review.pdf (last visited Sept. 9, 2018).

96. SEC Staff, Report on Modernization and Simplification of Regulation S-K as Required by Section 72003 of the Fixing America's Surface Transportation Act (Nov. 23, 2016), at https://www.sec.gov/files/sec-fast-act-report-2016.pdf (last visited Sept. 9, 2018).

97. Business and Financial Disclosure Required by Regulation S-K, SEC Release No. 33-10064 (Apr. 13, 2016)

98. Request for Comment on the Effectiveness of Financial Disclosures About Entities Other Than The Registrant, SEC Release No. 33-9929 (Sept. 25, 2015).

99. Disclosure Update and Simplification, SEC Release No. 33-10532 (Aug. 17, 2018).

100. *Id.* at 71.

requirements "differ in certain respects."[101] This may give issuers pause about continuing the common practice of merely cross-referencing their loss contingency disclosures in their Item 103 disclosures.

In addition, on October 11, 2017, the SEC issued proposed rule amendments, in a release titled "FAST Act Modernization and Simplification of Regulation S-K," which "are intended to modernize and simplify certain disclosure requirements in Regulation S-K, and related rules and forms, in a manner that reduces the costs and burdens on registrants while continuing to provide all material information to investors."[102] For example, the SEC proposes amending the instructions to Item 303(a), Management Discussion and Analysis of Financial Condition and Results of Operations ("MD&A"). Current instruction 303(a) states: "Generally, the discussion shall cover the three-year period covered by the financial statements and shall use year-to-year comparisons or any other formats that in the registrant's judgment enhance a reader's instruction."[103] As proposed, this sentence would be changed to the following: "Generally, the discussion shall cover the periods covered by the financial statements included in the filing and the registrant may use any presentation that in the registrant's judgment enhances a reader's understanding."[104] As explained by the SEC, this proposal is "intended to encourage companies to re-evaluate disclosures in their prior year MD&A and take a 'fresh look' to determine whether such disclosure remains material."[105] The SEC also proposes eliminating the list of examples of risk factor disclosures in Item 503(c),[106] in order to "encourage registrants to focus on their own risk identification process."[107] The SEC has not yet adopted final rules based on that proposal.

The disclosure effectiveness review is ongoing. In recent Congressional testimony, SEC Chairman Jay Clayton emphasized its importance: "Another important component of improving our public company regulatory regime is Corporation Finance's initiative to improve public company disclosure by reviewing our disclosure requirements and considering ways to improve the disclosure regime for the benefit of both investors and companies."[108]

---

101. *Id.* at 90. For a chart detailing the differences between Item 103 legal proceedings disclosures and GAAP loss contingency disclosures, see SEC Release No. 33-10110, at 100-02 (July 13, 2016).

102. FAST Act Modernization and Simplification of Regulation S-K, SEC Release No. 33-10425 (Oct. 11, 2017).

103. 17 C.F.R. § 229.303(a) instruction 303(a).

104. FAST Act Modernization and Simplification of Regulation S-K, SEC Release No. 33-10425, at 180 (Oct. 11, 2017).

105. *Id.* at 20.

106. 17 C.F.R. § 229.503(c). Note that the SEC also proposes relocating Item 503(c) to Subpart 100 of Regulation S-K.

107. FAST Act Modernization and Simplification of Regulation S-K, SEC Release No. 33-10425, at 49 (Oct. 11, 2017).

108. Chairman Jay Clayton, Testimony on "Oversight of the U.S. Securities and Exchange Commission" before the House Committee on Financial Services (June 21, 2018), at

B.   Quarterly Financial Reporting

A current hot topic is whether public companies should continue to be required to report earnings every quarter. On August 17, 2018, President Trump issued the following tweet:

> In speaking with some of the world's top business leaders I asked what it is that would make business (jobs) even better in the U.S. "Stop quarterly reporting & go to a six month system," said one. That would allow greater flexibility & save money. I have asked the SEC to study!

Later that day, Chairman Jay Clayton issued the following statement indicating that the SEC is studying the frequency of reporting requirements as part of its disclosure effectiveness review:

> The President has highlighted a key consideration for American companies and, importantly, American investors and their families—encouraging long-term investment in our country. Many investors and market participants share this perspective on the importance of long-term investing. Recently, the SEC has implemented—and continues to consider—a variety of regulatory changes that encourage long-term capital formation while preserving and, in many instances, enhancing key investor protections. In addition, the SEC's Division of Corporation Finance continues to study public company reporting requirements, including the frequency of reporting. As always, the SEC welcomes input from companies, investors, and other market participants as our staff considers these important matters.[109]

This policy debate will be interesting to follow. On the one hand, reducing the frequency of mandatory reporting would arguably reduce reporting costs and reduce the pressure on companies to focus on short-term results.[110] On the other hand, reducing the frequency of mandatory reporting would increase information asymmetry, thus potentially increasing the prevalence of insider trading and decreasing liquidity and efficiency.[111]

---

https://www.sec.gov/news/testimony/testimony-oversight-us-securities-and-exchange-commission (last visited Sept. 10, 2018).

109. Public Statement of Chairman Jay Clayton, Statement on Investing in America for the Long Term (Aug. 17, 2018), at https://www.sec.gov/news/public-statement/statement-clayton-081718 (last visited Sept. 10, 2018).

110. *But see* John C. Coffee, Jr., *What Really Drives "Short-Termism"?*, THE CLS BLUE SKY BLOG (Aug. 27, 2018), at http://clsbluesky.law.columbia.edu/2018/08/27/what-really-drives-short-termism/ (last visited Sept. 10, 2018) (suggesting that a shift to six-month reporting might exacerbate the problem of short-termism by increasing the pressure to meet earning targets).

111. Joshua R. Mitts, *Quarterly Reporting and Market Liquidity*, THE CLS BLUE SKY BLOG (Aug. 27, 2018), at http://clsbluesky.law.columbia.edu/2018/08/27/quarterly-reporting-and-market-liquidity/#_edn7 (last visited Sept. 10, 2018) ("While proponents of ending quarterly reporting point to the dangers of short-termism, less frequent disclosure is also likely to lead

As discussed by Professor John C. Coffee, Jr., perhaps the best course of action would be to retain quarterly reporting but discourage quarterly guidance: "Probably the simplest and best answer would be for financial managers to give less guidance about future earnings. Once a financial manager makes a forecast, he has effectively pledged his reputation and needs to protect it by manipulating earnings. Hence, less in the way of earnings forecasts implies less pressure on managers."[112] Indeed, Jamie Dimon and Warren E. Buffett expressed the same view in a recent *Wall St. Journal* opinion piece:

> [T]oday, together with Business Roundtable, an association of nearly 200 chief executive officers from major U.S. companies, we are encouraging all public companies to consider moving away from providing quarterly earnings-per-share guidance. In our experience, quarterly earnings guidance often leads to an unhealthy focus on short-term profits at the expense of long-term strategy, growth and sustainability.[113]

Citing the importance of transparency about financial and operating results, Dimon and Buffett clarified that their "views on quarterly earnings forecasts should not be misconstrued as opposition to quarterly and annual reporting."[114]

C. Pay Ratio Disclosure

Section 953(b) of the Dodd-Frank Act required the SEC to adopt a rule requiring reporting issuers to disclose the following information:

> (A) the median of the annual total compensation of all employees of the issuer, except the chief executive officer (or any equivalent position of the issuer);

---

to a decline in liquidity and to greater trading costs. The SEC should carefully consider the effect of increasing asymmetry on the flow of investment capital in secondary markets. . . . The presence of a robust, liquid market for a firm's shares reassures employees that equity-linked compensation can be readily converted to cash in the event of an unexpected financial shock. Greater trading strengthens the incentive to ferret out information about a firm and profit by arbitraging away temporary mispricing—thereby making prices more accurate. In short, quarterly reporting makes markets more efficient.").

112. John C. Coffee, Jr., *What Really Drives "Short-Termism"?*, THE CLS BLUE SKY BLOG (Aug. 27, 2018), at http://clsbluesky.law.columbia.edu/2018/08/27/what-really-drives-short-termism/ (last visited Sept. 10, 2018).

113. Jamie Dimon & Warren E. Buffett, *Short-Termism Is Harming the Economy*, WALL ST. J., June 7, 2018, at A17.

114. *Id.*

(B) the annual total compensation of the chief executive officer (or any equivalent position) of the issuer; and

(C) the ratio of the amount described in subparagraph (A) to the amount described in subparagraph (B).[115]

The Jumpstart Our Business Startups Act of 2012 excluded emerging growth companies from the pay ratio disclosure requirement.[116] On August 5, 2015, the SEC adopted a final rule implementing the pay ratio disclosure requirement, which required registrants to provide this disclosure for the first fiscal year beginning on or after January 1, 2017.[117] On February 6, 2017, Acting Chairman Michael S. Piwowar issued a public statement, titled "Reconsideration of Pay Ratio Rule Implementation," seeking public comment "on any unexpected challenges that issuers have experienced as they prepare for compliance with the rule and whether relief is needed."[118] In response to the feedback received, on September 21, 2017, the SEC issued "Commission Guidance on Pay Ratio Disclosure."[119] The SEC did not delay implementation of the pay ratio disclosure requirement, but it provided guidance on the "use of reasonable estimates, assumptions, and methodologies and statistical sampling" in order to identify the median employee and to calculate that employee's annual total compensation; the "use of existing internal records, such as tax or payroll records" to identify the median employee and his or her compensation; and the differentiation of "independent contractors" from "employees."[120] Simultaneously, the SEC staff published guidance "in order to assist registrants in determining how to use statistical sampling methodologies and other reasonable methods."[121]

Therefore, issuers began reporting their pay ratio disclosures in calendar year 2018. For example, here is Amazon.com, Inc.'s pay ratio disclosure:

> The 2017 annual total compensation of our median compensated employee other than Mr. Bezos was $28,446; Mr. Bezos' 2017 annual total compensation was $1,681,840, and the ratio of those amounts is 1-to-59. For purposes of identifying the median compensated employee, we took into account salary, bonus, and grant date fair value of RSUs [restricted stock units] granted

---

115. Dodd-Frank Wall Street Reform and Consumer Protection Act, Pub. Law No. 111-203, § 953(b), 124 Stat. 1376 (July 21, 2010).

116. *Id.* at § 102(a)(3).

117. Pay Ratio Disclosure, SEC Release No. 33-9877 (Aug. 5, 2015).

118. Public Statement of Acting Chairman Michael S. Piwowar, Reconsideration of Pay Ratio Rule Implementation, at https://www.sec.gov/news/statement/reconsideration-of-pay-ratio-rule-implementation.html (Feb. 6, 2017) (last visited Sept. 23, 2018).

119. Commission Guidance on Pay Ratio Disclosure, SEC Release No. 33-10415 (Sept. 21, 2017).

120. *Id.*

121. Division of Corporation Finance Guidance on Calculation of Pay Ratio Disclosure (Sept. 21, 2017), at https://www.sec.gov/corpfin/announcement/guidance-calculation-pay-ratio-disclosure (last visited Sept. 23, 2018).

during the year for all our employees as of December 31, 2017. We annualized this compensation for employees who did not work the entire year, except for employees designated as seasonal or temporary.[122]

Various consultants and researchers have issued reports analyzing this first set of pay ratio disclosures. For example, Pearl Meyer, Main Data Group, and the National Association of Corporate Directors issued a report analyzing pay ratio disclosures overall, by industry, by size of company, by number of employees, by percentage of non-U.S. workforce, by total shareholder return, and by CEO tenure.[123] The report includes the following takeaways:

- Pay ratios were not as high as anticipated (144:1 on average) and median employee pay was not nearly as low as anticipated (approximately $81,000 on average).
- Pay ratios were closely correlated with industry, with those in consumer discretionary at the top end (384:1) and those in utilities at the bottom end (59:1).
- Pay ratios were correlated with revenues and employee population (the higher the revenues/more employees, the higher the ratio).[124]

D.   Political Spending Disclosure

In the wake of *Citizens United v. Federal Election Commission*, in which the Supreme Court held that federal restrictions on corporate independent spending in support of or opposition to political candidates are unconstitutional,[125] a hot topic has been whether public companies should be required to disclose their political spending to shareholders. On August 3, 2011, the Committee on Disclosure of Corporate Political Spending, composed of ten academics, submitted a petition for rulemaking to the SEC, requesting that the SEC initiate a rulemaking project

---

122. Schedule 14A Proxy Statement, Amazon.com, Inc. (filed on April 18, 2018).
123. Pearl Meyer, Main Data Group, & National Association of Corporate Directors, Research Report, The CEO Pay Ratio: Data and Perspectives from the 2018 Proxy Season, at   https://www.pearlmeyer.com/ceo-pay-ratio-data-and-perspectives-2018-proxy-season.pdf (Sept. 2018) (last visited Sept. 23, 2018).
124. *Id.* at 14. See the full report for additional takeaways and analysis.
125. Citizens United v. Fed. Election Comm'n, 558 U.S. 310, 365 (2010) ("[T]he Government may not suppress political speech on the basis of the speaker's corporate identity.").

to require disclosure of corporate political spending to public-company shareholders.[126] To date, the petition has generated more than 1 million comments.[127]

The SEC has not initiated a rulemaking project, however. Congress funds the SEC, and since 2015, Congress has attached the following so-called "poison pill rider" to its appropriations bills prohibiting such rulemaking:

> None of the funds made available by this Act shall be used by the Securities and Exchange Commission to finalize, issue, or implement any rule, regulation, or order regarding the disclosure of political contributions, contributions to tax exempt organizations, or dues paid to trade associations.[128]

It is unknown whether, absent such a rider, the SEC would initiate rulemaking on this issue.

E. Environmental, Social, and Governance Disclosure

Scholars have continued to argue for rulemaking requiring enhanced environmental, social, and governance ("ESG") disclosure. Most recently, on October 1, 2018, Professors Cynthia A. Williams and Jill E. Fisch submitted a petition for SEC rulemaking on ESG disclosure.[129] Therein, they set out the following six arguments in support of the petition:

> (1) The SEC has clear statutory authority to require disclosure ESG information, and doing so will promote market efficiency, protect the competitive position of American public companies and the U.S. capital markets, and enhance capital formation;
>
> (2) ESG information is material to a broad range of investors today;

---

126. Petition to Require Public Companies to Disclose to Shareholders the Use of Corporate Resources for Political Activities, File No. 4-627 (Aug. 3, 2011), at https://www.sec.gov/rules/petitions/2011/petn4-637.pdf (last visited Sept. 23, 2018).

127. Comments on Rulemaking Petition: Petition to Require Public Companies to Disclose to Shareholders the Use of Corporate Resources for Political Activities, at https://www.sec.gov/comments/4-637/4-637.shtml (last visited Sept. 23, 2018).

128. *See* Consolidated Appropriations Act, 2018, Pub. L. No. 115-141, § 631 (March 23, 2018). The 2019 financial services appropriations bill, which is still in conference committee as of Oct. 15, 2018, contains the same rider. *See* H.R.6147 § 629.

129. Request for Rulemaking on Environmental, Social, and Governance (ESG) Disclosure, File No. 4-730 (Oct. 1, 2018) (submitted by Cynthia A. Williams, Osler Chair in Business Law, Osgoode Hall Law School & Jill E. Fisch, Saul A. Fox Distinguished Professor of Business Law, University of Pennsylvania Law School), at https://www.sec.gov/rules/petitions/2018/petn4-730.pdf (last visited Oct. 13, 2018). The petition included 65 additional signatories, including this author.

(3) Companies struggle to provide investors with ESG information that is relevant, reliable, and decision-useful;

(4) Companies' voluntary ESG disclosure is episodic, incomplete, incomparable, and inconsistent, and ESG disclosure in required SEC filings is similarly inadequate;

(5) Commission rulemaking will reduce the current burden on public companies and provide a level playing field for the many American companies engaging in voluntary ESG disclosure; and

(6) Petitions and stakeholder engagement seeking different kinds of ESG information suggest, in aggregate, that it is time for the SEC to regulate in this area.[130]

Under the SEC Rules of Practice, upon receipt of a petition for rulemaking, the Secretary of the Commission shall "refer it to the appropriate division or office for consideration and recommendation."[131]

VI. Section 10(b) of the Securities Exchange Act and Rule 10b-5

The securities laws' primary antifraud provision, § 10(b) of the Exchange Act and Rule 10b-5 promulgated thereunder, has continued to evolve in the courts over the past year, with important developments on the contours of scheme liability, the availability of the presumptions of reliance, the territorial scope of the securities fraud prohibition, and the "personal benefit" test for purposes of insider trading liability.

A. Scheme Liability

Rule 10b-5, promulgated under § 10(b) of the Securities Exchange Act,[132] contains three subparts:

It shall be unlawful for any person, directly or indirectly, by the use of any means or instrumentality of interstate commerce, or of the mails or of any facility of any national securities exchange,

(a) To employ any device, scheme, or artifice to defraud,

---

130. *Id.* at 2.
131. 17 C.F.R. § 201.192.
132. 15 U.S.C. § 78j(b).

(b) To make any untrue statement of a material fact or to omit to state a material fact necessary in order to make the statements made, in the light of the circumstances under which they were made, not misleading, or

(c) To engage in any act, practice, or course of business which operates or would operate as a fraud or deceit upon any person,

in connection with the purchase or sale of any security.[133]

In 2011, in *Janus Capital Group, Inc. v. First Derivative Traders*, the Supreme Court held that "the maker of a statement is the person or entity with ultimate authority over the statement, including its content and whether and how to communicate it."[134] Since then, lower courts have wrestled with whether, when an alleged fraud involves misstatements, defendants who do not satisfy the *Janus* test for maker liability can nonetheless be liable as primary violators of Rule 10b-5(a) and/or Rule 10b-5(c). This alternate theory of primary liability is often referred to as "scheme liability."

The Supreme Court will provide guidance on the contours of "scheme liability" during the 2018-2019 term in the case *Lorenzo v. SEC.*[135] The Court granted Lorenzo's petition for writ of certiorari on the following question:

The antifraud provisions of the federal securities laws prohibit two well-defined categories of misconduct. One category is the use of fraudulent statements in connection with the offer and sale of securities. The other category is employing fraudulent schemes in connection with the offer and sale of securities. In Janus Capital Group, Inc. v. First Derivative Traders, 564 U.S. 135 (2011), this Court considered the elements of a fraudulent statement claim and held that only the "maker" of a fraudulent statement may be held liable for that misstatement under Section 10(b) of the Securities Exchange Act of 1934 and SEC Rule 10b-5(b).

The question presented is whether a misstatement claim that does not meet the elements set forth in Janus can be repackaged and pursued as a fraudulent scheme claim. The Circuits have split 3-2 on this question. The Second, Eighth and Ninth Circuits have held that a misstatement alone cannot be the basis of a fraudulent scheme claim, while the DC Circuit and the Eleventh Circuit have held that a misstatement standing alone can be the basis of a fraudulent scheme claim.[136]

The D.C. Circuit panel who heard *Lorenzo v. SEC* issued a split decision, thus framing the arguments on both sides.[137] In an administrative

---

133. 17 C.F.R. § 240.10b-5.
134. Janus Capital Grp., Inc. v. First Derivative Traders, 564 U.S. 135, 142 (2011).
135. Lorenzo v. SEC., Petition for a Writ of Certiorari, No. 17-1077, 2018 WL 656234 (U.S. Jan. 26, 2018), cert. granted, 138 S. Ct. 2650 (2018).
136. *Id.*
137. Lorenzo v. SEC, 872 F.3d 578 (D.C. Cir. 2017), cert. granted, 138 S. Ct. 2650 (2018).

proceeding, the SEC found that Francis Lorenzo was a primary violator of § 10(b) and Rule 10b-5 because he sent materially misleading emails to potential investors. Francis Lorenzo contended, however, that "he sent the email messages at the behest of his boss, Gregg Lorenzo, and that Gregg Lorenzo supplied the content of the false statements, which Lorenzo copied and pasted into the messages before distributing them."[138] Under these facts, all of the judges on the panel agreed that Francis Lorenzo was not a "maker" under *Janus*.[139]

The majority held, however, that Francis Lorenzo could nonetheless be liable as a primary violator of Rule 10b-5(a) and Rule 10b-5(c), because "he 'engaged' in a fraudulent 'act' and 'employed' a fraudulent 'device' when, with knowledge of the statements' falsity, he sent the statements to potential investors carrying his stamp of approval as investment banking director."[140] The majority rejected Lorenzo's contention that this interpretation would erode the distinction between primary and aiding-and-abetting liability, which was a policy concern informing the Supreme Court's restrictive interpretation of "maker" in *Janus*:

> To the extent the *Janus* Court's concerns about aiding-and-abetting liability in private actions under Rule 10b-5(b) should inform our interpretation of those other four provisions, the conduct at issue in *Janus* materially differs from Lorenzo's actions in this case. Janus involved an investment adviser that initially drafted false statements which an independent entity subsequently decided to disseminate to investors in its own name. The investment adviser's role in originally devising the statements was unknown to the investors who ultimately received them. The Court thus described the investment adviser's conduct as "an undisclosed act preceding the decision of an independent entity to make a public statement."
>
> In this case, by contrast, Lorenzo's role was not "undisclosed" to investors. The recipients were fully alerted to his involvement: Lorenzo sent the emails from his account and under his name, in his capacity as director of investment banking at Charles Vista. While Gregg Lorenzo supplied the content of the false statements for inclusion in Lorenzo's email messages, Lorenzo effectively vouched for the emails' contents and put his reputation on the line by listing his personal phone number and inviting the recipients to "call with any questions." Nor did the dissemination of the false statements to investors result only from the separate "decision of an independent entity." Lorenzo himself communicated with investors, directly emailing them misstatements about the debenture offering.

---

138. *Id.* at 587.
139. *Id.* at 588 & 601.
140. *Id.* at 595.

Unlike in *Janus*, therefore, the recipients of Lorenzo's emails were not exposed to the false information only through the intervening act of "another person." . . .

As a result, insofar as the *Janus* Court declined to bring the investment adviser's actions in that case within the fold of Rule 10b-5 because doing so might reach too many persons fairly considered to be aiders and abettors, the same is not true of Lorenzo's distinct conduct in this case. The Court's concern that "aiders and abettors would be almost nonexistent" if a private action under Rule 10b-5 reached "an undisclosed act preceding the decision of an independent entity to make a public statement," need not obtain in the case of a person's self-attributed communications sent directly to investors (and backed by scienter). Lorenzo's actions thus can form the basis of a violation of Rules 10b-5(a) and (c) (as well as Sections 10(b) and 17(a)(1)) while still leaving ample room for "distinction between those who are primarily liable . . . and those who are secondarily liable."[141]

The dissenting judge on the panel, then-Judge Brett Kavanaugh, disagreed with the majority that non-makers could be primarily liable for securities fraud involving mere misstatements or omissions and criticized the SEC for overreaching:

The majority opinion creates a circuit split by holding that mere misstatements, standing alone, may constitute the basis for so-called scheme liability under the securities laws—that is, willful participation in a scheme to defraud—even if the defendant did not make the misstatements. No other court of appeals has adopted the approach that the majority opinion adopts here. Other courts have instead concluded that scheme liability must be based on conduct that goes beyond a defendant's role in preparing mere misstatements or omissions made by others. *See, e.g., Public Pension Fund Group v. KV Pharmaceutical Co.,* 679 F.3d 972, 987 (8th Cir. 2012); *WPP Luxembourg Gamma Three Sarl v. Spot Runner, Inc.,* 655 F.3d 1039, 1057 (9th Cir. 2011); *Lentell v. Merrill Lynch & Co.,* 396 F.3d 161, 177 (2d Cir. 2005); *see also SEC v. Kelly,* 817 F. Supp. 2d 340, 343-44 (S.D.N.Y. 2011). Otherwise, the SEC would be able to evade the important statutory distinction between primary liability and secondary (aiding and abetting) liability. After all, if those who aid and abet a misstatement are themselves primary violators for engaging in a scheme to defraud, what would be the point of the distinction between primary and secondary liability?

The distinction between primary and secondary liability matters, particularly for private securities lawsuits. For decades, however, the SEC has tried to erase that distinction so as to expand the scope of primary liability under the securities laws. For decades, the Supreme Court has pushed back hard against the SEC's attempts to unilaterally rewrite the law. *See Janus,* 564 U.S. 135; *Stoneridge Investment Partners, LLC v. Scientific-Atlanta, Inc.,* 552 U.S. 148 (2008); *Central Bank of Denver, N.A. v. First Interstate Bank of Denver, N.A.,* 511 U.S. 164 (1994).

---

141. *Id.* at 590-91 (citations omitted).

Still undeterred in the wake of that body of Supreme Court precedent, the SEC has continued to push the envelope and has tried to circumvent those Supreme Court decisions. *See, e.g., In the Matter of John P. Flannery & James D. Hopkins,* Release No. 3981 (Dec. 15, 2014). This case is merely the latest example.

I agree with the other courts that have rejected the SEC's persistent efforts to end-run the Supreme Court. I therefore respectfully disagree with the majority opinion that Lorenzo's role in forwarding the alleged misstatements made by Lorenzo's boss can be the basis for scheme liability against Lorenzo.[142]

Interestingly, each of the cases that Judge Kavanaugh's dissent cites as an example of the Supreme Court "pushing] back hard against the SEC's attempts to unilaterally rewrite the law" involved private securities litigation, not an SEC enforcement action. Now-Justice Kavanaugh has committed to recuse himself from hearing any case in which he was involved as a judge,[143] so he will not participate in the Supreme Court's decision in *Lorenzo.*

As foreshadowed in the majority and dissenting opinions discussed above, this case will be especially impactful in private securities litigation because, unlike the SEC, private litigants cannot assert claims against mere aiders and abettors.[144] If the Supreme Court holds that non-makers can nonetheless be liable as primary violators with respect to misstatements or omissions under a scheme liability theory, it will potentially expand the scope of liable defendants in private civil securities litigation.

B.   Presumptions of Reliance

Reliance is an element of a private cause of action for securities fraud under § 10(b) of the Securities Exchange Act[145] and Rule 10b-5[146] promulgated thereunder.[147] If each member of a plaintiff class had to show individualized reliance on a defendant's alleged misrepresentation, the class could not be certified because "questions of law or fact common to class members" would not "predominate over any questions affecting only individual members."[148] Two presumptions of class-wide reliance are potentially available, however, thus permitting class certification.

---

142. *Id.* at 600-01 (Kavanaugh, J., dissenting) (citations shortened).

143. Questionnaire for Nominee to the Supreme Court, submitted by Brett Kavanaugh to the United States Senate Committee on the Judiciary, p. 109, at https://www.judiciary.senate. gov/imo/media/doc/Brett%20M.%20Kavanaugh%20SJQ%20(PUBLIC).pdf (last visited Sept. 23, 2018).

144. Central Bank of Denver, N.A. v. First Interstate Bank of Denver, N.A., 511 U.S. 164, 177-78 (1994).

145. 15 U.S.C. § 78j(b).

146. 17 C.F.R. § 240.10b-5.

147. Halliburton Co. v. Erica P. John Fund, Inc., 134 S. Ct. 2398, 2407 (2014) ("*Halliburton II*").

148. FED. R. CIV. P. 23(b)(3).

First, in *Affiliated Ute Citizens of Utah v. United States*, the Supreme Court held that a presumption of reliance applies in omissions cases:

> Under the circumstances of this case, involving primarily a failure to disclose, positive proof of reliance is not a prerequisite to recovery. All that is necessary is that the facts withheld be material in the sense that a reasonable investor might have considered them important in the making of this decision. This obligation to disclose and this withholding of a material fact establish the requisite element of causation in fact.[149]

As later explained by the Court, "[r]equiring a plaintiff to show a speculative state of facts, *i.e.*, how he would have acted if omitted material information had been disclosed . . . would place an unnecessarily unrealistic evidentiary burden on the Rule 10b-5 plaintiff who has traded on an impersonal market."[150]

Second, the fraud-on-the-market presumptions of reliance, first recognized by the Supreme Court in *Basic Inc. v. Levinson*,[151] has two essential components. First, an alleged misrepresentation has a price impact because material "public information generally affects stock prices."[152] Second, most investors who purchase at the market price do so in reliance on the integrity of market price,[153] thus indirectly relying on the alleged misrepresentation itself.[154] At class certification, plaintiffs can show these two components of the fraud-on-the-market presumption of reliance by invoking two constituent presumptions. First, in order to invoke a presumption of price impact, plaintiffs must establish the following two prerequisites by a preponderance of the evidence: (1) that the alleged material misrepresentation was publicly disseminated; and (2) that the market was efficient.[155] Second, in order to invoke a presumption that the plaintiff class purchased the securities in reliance on the integrity of the market price, plaintiffs must show that investors "purchased the stock at the market price during the relevant period."[156] At class certification, defendants can prevent the invocation of the fraud-on-the-market presumption of reliance by demonstrating that plaintiffs failed to establish these prerequisites (with the exception of materiality[157]). If plaintiffs successfully invoke the fraud-on-the-market presumption of reliance, defendants can rebut each constituent presumption

---

149. Affiliated Ute Citizens of Utah v. United States, 406 U.S. 128, 153-54 (1972).
150. Basic Inc. v. Levinson, 485 U.S. 224, 245 (1988).
151. *Id.* at 250.
152. *Halliburton II*, 134 S. Ct. at 2410.
153. *Id.* at 2410-11.
154. *Basic*, 485 U.S. at 247.
155. *Halliburton II*, 134 S. Ct. at 2414.
156. *Id.*
157. Amgen Inc. v. Connecticut Retirement Plans & Trust Funds, 568 U.S. 455, 474 (2013).

at the merits stage.[158] In addition, in *Halliburton Co. v. Erica P. John Fund, Inc.* (*"Halliburton II"*), the Supreme Court held that defendants can rebut the first component of the presumption—price impact—at the class certification stage.[159] Thus, after *Halliburton II*, "[d]efendants may seek to defeat the *Basic* presumption at that [class certification] stage through direct as well as indirect price impact evidence."[160]

In the wake of *Halliburton II*, courts have struggled with two issues: (1) the parameters for when an alleged fraud can be classified as an omissions case, rather than a misstatements case, so as to invoke the *Affiliated Ute* presumption of reliance, which does not rely on price impact; and (2) the defendants' burdens of production and persuasion when seeking to rebut the presumption of price impact at the class certification stage.[161]

The Second Circuit recently addressed both of these issues in *Waggoner v. Barclays PLC*.[162] The plaintiffs, on behalf of investors who purchased American Depository Shares of Barclays PLC during the class period, asserted claims under § 10(b) and Rule 10b-5 against Barclays related to its communications about Barclays' Liquidity Cross ("LX"), the alternate trading system that it operated through an American subsidiary. In particular, the plaintiffs alleged that Barclays made false statements and omissions about the efforts it was taking to prevent high-frequency traders from front-running in LX. The Second Circuit summarized the plaintiffs' allegations as follows:

> The Plaintiffs alleged that Barclays' statements about LX and Liquidity Profiling "were materially false and misleading by omission or otherwise because," contrary to its assertions, "Barclays did not in fact protect clients from aggressive high frequency trading activity, did not restrict predatory traders' access to other clients," and did not "eliminate traders who continued to behave in a predatory manner."

> According to the complaint, Barclays "did not monitor client orders continuously," or even apply Liquidity Profiling "to a significant portion of the trading" conducted in LX. Instead, the Plaintiffs alleged that Barclays "favored high frequency traders" by giving them information about LX that was not available to other investors and applying "overrides" that allowed such traders to be given a Liquidity Profiling rating more favorable than the one they should have received.[163]

---

158. *Basic*, 485 U.S. at 248-49.
159. *Halliburton II*, 134 S. Ct. at 2417.
160. *Id.* at 2417.
161. Meyer Eisenberg, *Halliburton II: Where Do We Go From Here?*, THE CLS BLUE SKY BLOG (July 10, 2014), at http://clsbluesky.law.columbia.edu/2014/07/10/8667/ (last visited Sept. 23, 2018) ("The Court clearly reaffirms the *Basic* opportunity for the defendants to rebut the presumption of reliance at certification. By what standard?").
162. Waggoner v. Barclays PLC, 875 F.3d 79 (2d Cir. 2017).
163. *Id.* at 88 (citations omitted).

The district court granted the plaintiffs' motion for class certification, concluding that the *Affiliated Ute* presumption applied and that, in the alternative, the *Basic* presumption of reliance applied. Barclays appealed the class certification order.

First, relying on the Supreme Court's reasoning in *Affiliated Ute* and prior Second Circuit precedent interpreting *Affiliated Ute*, the Second Circuit held that the *Affiliated Ute* presumption did not apply:

> The Defendants first argue that the district court erred by concluding that the *Affiliated Ute* presumption applies because the Plaintiffs' complaint is based primarily on allegations of affirmative misrepresentations, not omissions. We agree.

> When the Supreme Court first recognized the *Affiliated Ute* presumption, it explained that under the circumstances of that case, a case "involving *primarily a failure to disclose,* positive proof of reliance is not a prerequisite to recovery." *Affiliated Ute,* 406 U.S. at 153 (emphasis added). We later determined that the presumption was inapplicable in two cases because the claims of fraud at issue were not based primarily on omissions. Those decisions are particularly helpful in discerning whether the allegations here principally concern misrepresentations or omissions.

> In the first, *Wilson v. Comtech Telecommunications Corp.,* 648 F.2d 88 (2d Cir. 1981), we cautioned that the labels "misrepresentation" and "omission" "are of little help" because in "many instances, an omission to state a material fact relates back to an earlier statement, and if it is reasonable to think that that prior statement still stands, then the omission may also be termed a misrepresentation." We explained that what "is important is to understand the rationale for a presumption of causation in fact in cases like *Affiliated Ute,* in which no positive statements exist: reliance as a practical matter is impossible to prove." In *Wilson,* the president of the defendant corporation made sales and earnings projections at a conference of investors and securities analysts. Several months later, those projections were shown to be materially inaccurate. The earlier projections became misleading when subsequent corrective information was not timely disclosed. In other words, as we explain in somewhat more detail, the projections eventually became "half-truths." Unlike in *Affiliated Ute,* however, in *Wilson* the omissions alone were not the actionable events and proving reliance on them was therefore not "impossible"; accordingly, we concluded that the plaintiff was required to demonstrate that he relied on the earlier misrepresentations in executing his stock purchases.

> Similarly, in *Starr ex rel. Estate of Sampson v. Georgeson Shareholder, Inc.,* 412 F.3d 103 (2d Cir. 2005), we concluded that the *Affiliated Ute* presumption did not apply because the plaintiffs' claims in that case were "not 'primarily' omission claims." We explained that the plaintiffs' claims there, as in *Wilson,* focused on "misleading statements" that were not corrected. The plaintiffs asserted that the omissions only "exacerbated the misleading nature of the affirmative statements."

In this case, the *Affiliated Ute* presumption does not apply for the same reasons that it was inapplicable in *Wilson* and *Starr*. First, the Plaintiffs' complaint alleges numerous affirmative misstatements by the Defendants. The Plaintiffs are therefore not in a situation in which it is impossible for them to point to affirmative misstatements. Second, the Plaintiffs focus their claims on those affirmative misstatements. In arguing that class certification was proper, for example, the Plaintiffs stated that Barclays had "touted LX as a safe trading venue" and "consistently assured the public that its dark pool was a model of transparency and integrity."

Indeed, the omissions the Plaintiffs list in their complaint are directly related to the earlier statements Plaintiffs also claim are false. For example, the Plaintiffs argue that Barclays failed to disclose that Liquidity Profiling did not apply to a significant portion of the trades conducted in LX. That "omission" is simply the inverse of the Plaintiffs' misrepresentation allegation: Barclays' statement that Liquidity Profiling protected LX traders was false. Thus, as alleged in *Starr*, the omissions here "exacerbated the misleading nature of the affirmative statements." The *Affiliated Ute* presumption does not apply to earlier misrepresentations made more misleading by subsequent omissions, or to what has been described as "half-truths," nor does it apply to misstatements whose only omission is the truth that the statement misrepresents.[164]

Second, the Second Circuit addressed the defendants' burdens of production and persuasion on the lack of price impact in order to rebut the fraud-on-market presumption of reliance once the plaintiffs have established the prerequisites for invoking the presumption:

> We now turn to the Defendants' argument that the district court erred by shifting the burden of persuasion, rather than the burden of production, to rebut the *Basic* presumption. . . .

> It would be inconsistent with *Halliburton II* to require that plaintiffs meet this evidentiary burden while allowing defendants to rebut the *Basic* presumption by simply producing some evidence of market inefficiency, but not demonstrating its inefficiency to the district court. The presumption of reliance would also be of little value if it were so easily overcome. Both in *Basic* and again in *Halliburton II*, the Supreme Court recognized the importance of the presumption of reliance in putative class actions where, without such a presumption, there would be "'an unnecessarily unrealistic evidentiary burden on the Rule 10b-5 plaintiff who has traded on an impersonal market.'"

> Quoting *Basic*, the *Halliburton II* Court also explained that the showing to sever the link between the misrepresentation and the price received or paid would rebut the *Basic* presumption "because 'the basis for finding that the fraud had been transmitted through market price would be gone.'" . . . A concurring opinion in *Halliburton II* by Justice Ginsburg and joined by Justices

---

164. *Id.* at 95-96 (some citations omitted and other citations shortened).

Breyer and Sotomayor stated that the majority recognized "that it is incumbent upon the defendant to show the absence of price impact."

This Supreme Court guidance indicates that defendants seeking to rebut the *Basic* presumption must demonstrate a lack of price impact by a preponderance of the evidence at the class certification stage rather than merely meet a burden of production.

. . .

Apart from their arguments that *Basic* and *Halliburton II* do not support the conclusion that it is a burden of persuasion that applies to defendants attempting to rebut the *Basic* presumption at the class certification stage, the Defendants have relied on Federal Rule of Evidence 301 in arguing that it is merely a burden of production that is placed upon defendants. Rule 301 provides:

> In a civil case, unless a federal statute or these rules provide otherwise, the party against whom a presumption is directed has the burden of producing evidence to rebut the presumption. But this rule does not shift the burden of persuasion, which remains on the party who had it originally.

Fed. R. Evid. 301.

The Defendants assert that because no federal statute or other rule of evidence "provide[s] otherwise," we are required to conclude that defendants bear only the burden of producing evidence when they seek to rebut the *Basic* presumption. We disagree.

The *Basic* presumption was adopted by the Supreme Court pursuant to federal securities laws. Thus, there is a sufficient link to those statutes to meet Rule 301's statutory element requirement. . . .

In *Halliburton II* the Supreme Court stated that "[a]lthough the [*Basic*] presumption is a judicially created doctrine designed to implement a judicially created cause of action, we have described the presumption as a substantive doctrine of federal securities-fraud law." Rule 301 therefore imposes no impediment to our conclusion that the burden of persuasion, not production, to rebut the *Basic* presumption shifts to defendants.[165]

Defendants' burdens of production and persuasion when rebutting price impact at class certification have not yet been directly addressed by the Supreme Court. The Eighth Circuit has cited Federal Rule of Evidence 301 when discussing defendants' rebuttal of the presumption of price impact at class certification,[166] and the author of this book has argued that,

---

165. *Id.* at 99-103 (citations omitted).
166. IBEW Local 98 Pension Fund v. Best Buy Co., 818 F.3d 775, 782 (8th Cir. 2016) ("We agree with the district court that, when plaintiffs presented a *prima facie* case that the *Basic* presumption applies to their claims, defendants had the burden to come forward with evidence showing a lack of price impact. *See* FED. R. EVID. 301 ('the party against whom a presumption is directed has the burden of producing evidence to rebut the presumption').").

contrary to the Second Circuit's holding in *Waggoner*, Rule 301 applies in this context.[167]

C. Territorial Scope

In 2010, in *Morrison v. National Australia Bank Ltd.*, the Supreme Court held that § 10(b) does not overcome the presumption against extraterritoriality.[168] Section 10(b) states that it applies "in connection with the purchase or sale of any security registered on a national securities exchange or any security not so registered." Therefore, the *Morrison* Court limited the applicability of § 10(b) to "transactions in securities listed on domestic exchanges, and domestic transactions in other securities."[169] The holding in *Morrison* has led to several interpretive questions, which the lower courts have addressed.

The first prong of *Morrison*'s test uses the term "domestic exchanges," while § 10(b) uses the term "national securities exchanges," leading to the question of whether securities listed on a domestic exchange that is not a national securities exchange would be within the scope of § 10(b). In a recent opinion, although not resolving the issue because the subject securities were traded on the over-the-counter market rather than on an exchange, the Ninth Circuit suggested that securities listed on a domestic exchange, even if not a national securities exchange, would be within the scope of § 10(b):

> The Court derived its first category of transactions to which Section 10(b) applies from Section 10(b)'s language: "any security registered on a national securities exchange." 15 U.S.C. § 78j(b); *see Morrison*, 561 U.S. at 268 n.10 (stating that the second category arises from the other half of Section 10(b), "any security not so registered"). But when articulating the rule, the *Morrison* Court repeatedly describes the regulated category as "securities listed on *domestic* exchanges."

> Facially, the terms are distinct: "national security exchange" is a term of art referring to a *subset* of "exchanges" that are registered with the Securities and Exchange Commission and that abide by the requirements set out in 15 U.S.C. § 78f and its regulations. Twenty one exchanges are currently so registered, and two are exempt based on a limited volume of transactions. No over-the-counter market is a "national security exchange," and the Funds do not argue otherwise.

---

167. Wendy Gerwick Couture, *Answering* Halliburton II *'s Unanswered Question: Burdens of Production and Persuasion on Price Impact at Class Certification*, 43 Sec. Reg. L.J. 167 (2015).
168. Morrison v. Nat'l Aus. Bank Ltd., 561 U.S. 247, 265 (2010).
169. *Id.* at 267.

Toshiba urges us to eliminate any discrepancy by reading the term "domestic exchange" as used in *Morrison* as the equivalent of "national securities exchange." But Toshiba incorrectly characterizes *Morrison*'s discussion of "domestic exchange" as mere shorthand for what Toshiba believes the Court must have meant to write — national securities exchange. The Court uses the term "domestic exchange" interchangeably both when defining the first category of transactions to which Section 10(b) applies and throughout the remainder of the opinion. And there is little wonder that the Court did so: the entire focus of the *Morrison* opinion is the "longstanding principle" that Congressional legislation, including Section 10(b), is meant to apply only within the territorial jurisdiction of the United States, and its announcement of the "transactional test" to separate domestic from foreign purchases and sales.

We need not and do not resolve this argument, although from our reading the Funds have the better of it. The over-the-counter market on which Toshiba ADRs trade is simply not an "exchange" under the Exchange Act.[170]

The second prong of the *Morrison* test states that § 10(b) also applies to "domestic transactions in other securities," and the lower courts have sought to interpret when a transaction so qualifies. In 2012, in *Absolute Activist Value Master Fund Ltd. v. Ficeto*, the Second Circuit held "that a securities transaction is domestic when the parties incur irrevocable liability to carry out the transaction within the United States or when title is passed within the United States."[171] In 2015, the Third Circuit adopted the irrevocable liability test,[172] and in 2018, the Ninth Circuit adopted it as well:

We are persuaded by the Second and Third Circuits' analysis and therefore adopt the irrevocable liability test to determine whether the securities were the subject of a domestic transaction. Looking to where purchasers incurred the liability to take and pay for securities, and where sellers incurred the liability to deliver securities, *Absolute Activist*, 677 F.3d at 68, hews to Section 10(b)'s focus on transactions and *Morrison*'s instruction that purchases and sales constitute transactions, *Morrison*, 561 U.S. at 267-68. Furthermore, factual allegations concerning contract formation, placement of purchase orders, passing of title, and the exchange of money are directly related to the consummation of a securities transaction. *See Absolute Activist*, 677 F.3d at 70.[173]

---

170. Stoyas v. Toshiba Corp., 896 F.3d 933, 945 (9th Cir. 2018) (some citations shortened or omitted for clarity); *but see* United States v. Georgiou, 777 F.3d 125, 135 (3d Cir. 2015) (looking at "the list of registered national security exchanges on the SEC Webpage on Exchanges" in order to determine whether a transaction satisfied the first prong of the *Morrison* test).

171. Absolute Activist Value Master Fund Ltd. v. Ficeto, 677 F.3d 60, 69 (2d Cir. 2012).

172. United States v. Georgiou, 777 F.3d 125, 137 (3d Cir. 2015) ("We now hold that irrevocable liability establishes the location of a securities transaction.").

173. Stoyas v. Toshiba Corp., 896 F.3d 933, 949 (9th Cir. 2018) (citations shortened).

In 2014, however, the Second Circuit added a carve-out to the above "domestic transactions" test. In *Parkcentral Glob. Hub Ltd. v. Porsche Auto. Holdings SE*, the Second Circuit held that "a domestic transaction is necessary but not necessarily sufficient to make § 10(b) applicable" and that § 10(b) does not apply if the transaction is "so predominantly foreign as to be impermissibly extraterritorial."[174] In 2018, the Second Circuit reaffirmed this precedent,[175] but the Ninth Circuit rejected it,[176] creating a circuit split. When rejecting the *Parkcentral* carve-out, the Ninth Circuit reasoned as follows:

> But the principal reason that we should not follow the *Parkcentral* decision is because it is contrary to Section 10(b) and *Morrison* itself. It carves-out "predominantly foreign" securities fraud claims from Section 10(b)'s ambit, disregarding Section 10(b)'s text: the domestic "purchase or sale of *any* security registered on a national securities exchange or *any* security not so registered," 15 U.S.C. § 78j(b) (emphases added). The basis for the carve-out was speculation about Congressional intent, an inquiry *Morrison* rebukes. *Parkcentral's* test for whether a claim is foreign is an open-ended, under-defined multi-factor test, akin to the vague and unpredictable tests that *Morrison* criticized and endeavored to replace with a "clear," administrable rule. And *Parkcentral's* analysis relies heavily on the foreign location of the allegedly deceptive conduct, which *Morrison* held to be irrelevant to the Exchange Act's applicability, given Section 10(b)'s exclusive focus on transactions.[177]

Commentators have noted that, as a result of this split, "the Ninth Circuit has adopted a test that is in some ways narrower than the Second Circuit's, and that therefore may make it harder for foreign defendants to argue that domestic transactions in their securities do not satisfy *Morrison*."[178]

Finally, of note, even if the securities transactions at issue are domestic and thus within the scope of § 10(b) under *Morrison*, the defendant's allegedly fraudulent conduct must also be "in connection with" with the purchase or sale of such securities in order to be actionable under § 10(b).[179]

---

174. Parkcentral Glob. Hub Ltd. v. Porsche Auto. Holdings SE, 763 F.3d 198, 216 (2d Cir. 2014).

175. Giunta v. Dingman, 893 F.3d 73, 82 (2d Cir. 2018) (applying *Parkcentral*).

176. Stoyas v. Toshiba Corp., 896 F.3d 933, 950 (9th Cir. 2018).

177. *Id.* (citations omitted).

178. Jared Gerber, Leslie Silverman, Roger Cooper, & Adam Fleisher, *Circuit Split on* Morrison *Application*, Harvard Law School Forum on Corporate Governance and Financial Regulation (Aug. 12, 2018), at https://corpgov.law.harvard.edu/2018/08/12/circuit-split-on-morrison-application/ (last visited Sept. 24, 2018).

179. Stoyas v. Toshiba Corp., 896 F.3d 933, 950-51 (9th Cir. 2018) ("*Morrison* delineates the transactions to which the Exchange Act can theoretically apply without being impermissibly extraterritorial, but while applicability is necessary, it is not sufficient to state an Exchange Act claim. Section 10(b) of the Exchange Act makes it unlawful '[t]o use or employ, *in connection with* the purchase or sale' of a security 'any manipulative or deceptive device or contrivance.' Accordingly, there must be 'a connection between the misrepresentation or omission and the purchase or sale of a security.'") (citations omitted).

D. Insider Trading

In response to Supreme Court precedent, the Second Circuit's "personal benefit" test for purposes of tipper-tippee liability in the gift context has continued to evolve. As a reminder, in *Dirks v. SEC*,[180] the Supreme Court held that a tippee inherits a tipper's duty to disclose or abstain from trading only if the tipper "personally will benefit, directly or indirectly, from his disclosure."[181] The Court explained this personal benefit test as follows:

> This requires courts to focus on objective criteria, *i.e.*, whether the insider receives a direct or indirect personal benefit from the disclosure, such as a pecuniary gain or a reputational benefit that will translate into future earnings. . . . There are objective facts and circumstances that often justify such an inference. For example, there may be a relationship between the insider and the recipient that suggests a quid pro quo from the latter, or an intention to benefit the particular recipient. The elements of fiduciary duty and exploitation of nonpublic information also exists when an insider makes a gift of confidential information to a trading relative or friend. The tip and trade resemble trading by the insider himself followed by a gift of the profits to the recipient.[182]

In 2014, in *United States v. Newman*,[183] the Second Circuit interpreted the personal benefit test in the gift context in a restrictive manner:

> To the extent *Dirks* suggests that a personal benefit may be inferred from a personal relationship between the tipper and tippee, where the tippee's trades "resemble trading by the insider himself followed by a gift of the profits to the recipient," we hold that such an inference is impermissible in the absence of proof of a meaningfully close personal relationship that generates an exchange that is objective, consequential, and represents at least a potential gain of a pecuniary or similarly valuable nature. In other words, as Judge Walker noted in [*United States v.*] *Jiau*, this requires evidence of "a relationship between the insider and the recipient that suggests a *quid pro quo* from the latter, or an intention to benefit the [latter]."[184]

In 2016, in *Salman v. United States*,[185] the Supreme Court explicitly rejected the "pecuniary or similarly valuable nature" component of the *Newman* personal benefit test:

---

180. Dirks v. SEC, 463 U.S. 646 (1983).
181. *Id.* at 662.
182. *Id.* at 664.
183. United States v. Newman, 773 F.3d 438 (2d Cir. 2014).
184. *Id.* at 453 (quoting United States v. Jiau, 734 F.3d 147, 153 (3d Cir. 2013)).
185. Salman v. United States, 137 S. Ct. 420 (2016).

Dirks specifies that when a tipper gives inside information to a "trading relative or friend," the jury can infer that the tipper meant to provide the equivalent of a cash gift. In such situations, the tipper benefits personally because giving a gift of trading information is the same thing as trading by the tipper followed by a gift of the proceeds. . . . To the extent the Second Circuit held that the tipper must also receive something of a "pecuniary or similarly valuable nature" in exchange for a gift to family or friends, we agree with the Ninth Circuit that this requirement is inconsistent with *Dirks*.[186]

Post-*Salman*, the question before the Second Circuit was whether the "meaningfully close personal relationship" component of the *Newman* personal benefit test remained good law. Panel decisions, like *Newman*, remain binding precedent until they are overruled by an *en banc* panel or by the Supreme Court. A panel of the Second Circuit repeatedly wrestled with this question in *United States v. Martoma*, issuing one opinion in August 2017 ("*Martoma I*") and then issuing a superseding opinion in June 2018 ("*Martoma II*").[187]

In *Martoma I*, which was later superseded, a majority of the panel concluded that "*Salman* fundamentally altered the analysis underlying *Newman*'s 'meaningfully close personal relationship' requirement such that the 'meaningfully close personal relationship' requirement is no longer good law."[188] Judge Rosemary Pooler dissented, contending that *Salman* "left untouched the first holding that, in order to allow inference of a personal benefit, gifts must be exchanged within a 'meaningfully close personal relationship.'"[189]

Almost a year later, the panel issued a superseding opinion, *Martoma II*.[190] The majority, rather than concluding that *Newman*'s "meaningfully close personal relationship" test was no longer good law post-*Salman*, instead interpreted the test in the following expansive manner:

The term "meaningfully close personal relationship" is new to our insider trading jurisprudence, and, viewed in isolation, it might admit multiple interpretations. But *Newman* provided substantial guidance. Immediately after introducing the "meaningfully close personal relationship" concept, *Newman* held that it "requires evidence of 'a relationship between the insider and the recipient that suggests a *quid pro quo* from the latter, or an intention to benefit the [latter].'" As explained above, each of these is an independently sufficient basis to infer a personal benefit under *Dirks* and its progeny. In other

---

186. *Id.* at 428.
187. United States v. Martoma, 869 F.3d 58 (2d. Cir. 2017) ("Martoma I"), superseded by 894 F.3d 64 (2d Cir. 2018) ("Martoma II").
188. *Martoma I*, 869 F.3d at 69.
189. *Id.* at 82 (J. Poole, dissenting).
190. *Martoma II*, 894 F.3d 64.

words, *Newman* cabined the gift theory using two *other* freestanding personal benefits that have long been recognized by our case law.[191]

In short, the *Martoma II* majority interpreted *Newman* as identifying two independent avenues to satisfy the personal benefit test: (1) with evidence of a relationship between the tipper and the tippee that suggests a *quid pro quo* from the latter, or (2) with evidence of an intention to benefit the tippee. To exemplify the second avenue, the majority provided the following example of a gift of a tip to a stranger:

> For example, suppose a tipper discloses inside information to a perfect stranger and says, in effect, you can make a lot of money by trading on this. . . . [T]he statement "you can make a lot of money by trading on this," following the disclosure of material non-public information, suggests an intention to benefit the tippee in breach of the insider's fiduciary duty.[192]

Judge Pooler dissented again in *Martoma II*, critiquing the majority for "attempt[ing] to redefine 'meaningfully close personal relationship' in subjective rather than objective terms, rendering *Newman* a relic."[193] She further argued that "[o]nly by abrogating *Newman* could my colleagues announce a new rule that a jury can infer a personal benefit based on a freestanding 'intention to benefit' and that this 'intention to benefit' is at the core of the meaningfully close personal relationship standard."[194] Judge Pooler also responded to the majority's example of a gift of information to a stranger:

> They ask us to imagine a situation where a tipper "discloses inside information to a perfect stranger and says, in effect, you can make a lot of money by trading on this." Wouldn't it be absurd if this perfect stranger could not be held liable for insider trading if he went ahead and traded on this information? No, it would not be. At least, not if one takes the personal benefit rule seriously. Ex hypothesi, the fictional tipper in their scenario receives absolutely nothing in return for his disclosure, except, I suppose, the warmth that comes with knowing that somebody else might have made some money because of his actions (or perhaps the schadenfreude that comes with knowing that shareholders were defrauded). But if those sorts of "benefits" were enough, then every disclosure of inside information without affirmative indication of a pure heart would be presumptively beneficial to the tipper. *Dirks* rejected that possibility, and every appellate court to have considered the issue, including us, has consistently done the same. That is the law whether

---

191. *Id.* at 77.
192. *Id.* at 75.
193. *Id.* at 80 (J. Poole, dissenting).
194. *Id.* at 80-81 (J. Poole, dissenting).

we like or not, but, for what it's worth, I see no reason to worry that truly random acts of enrichment can go unpunished.[195]

As commentators have noted, "[f]or now, the Second Circuit's 'intention to benefit' inquiry in the gift-giving context provides the government some ammunition in asserting that the pecuniary gloss of *Newman* is limited, potentially aiding the government's prosecution of tipping cases."[196]

VII.   *Securities Class Action Practice and Procedure*

Most securities litigation proceeds as class actions, and the past year has seen significant Supreme Court opinions on the scope of the Securities Litigation Uniform Standards Act and on the availability of class action tolling. In addition, there has been renewed debate about the potential for mandatory arbitration of securities claims.

A.   Securities Litigation Uniform Standards Act

In the recent case of *Cyan v. Beaver County Employees Retirement Fund*, the Supreme Court clarified that the Securities Litigation Uniform Standards Act ("SLUSA")[197] does not deprive state courts of jurisdiction over class actions asserting only Securities Act claims, such as claims under § 11 or § 12(a)(2).[198]

As background, in 1995, Congress enacted the Private Securities Litigation Reform Act ("PSLRA"), which added substantive and procedural restrictions to claims asserted under the Securities Act and the Exchange Act.[199] In an effort to avoid the PSLRA's strictures, plaintiffs responded by bringing securities class actions in state court under state law. In 1998, in order to prevent plaintiffs from circumventing the PSLRA's restrictions in this manner, Congress enacted SLUSA, which included a state-law class action bar:

---

195. *Id.* at 86 (J. Poole, dissenting).

196. David Miller & Grant MacQueen, *Martoma—The Latest Critical Insider Trading Decision*, Law 360 (June 27, 2018), at https://www.law360.com/articles/1057759/martoma-the-latest-critical-insider-trading-decision (last visited Oct. 10, 2018).

197. Securities Litigation Uniform Standards Act of 1998, Pub. L. No. 105-353, 112 Stat 3227 (Nov. 3, 1998).

198. Cyan v. Beaver County Employees Retirement Fund, 138 S. Ct. 1061 (2018).

199. Private Securities Litigation Reform Act of 1995, Pub. L. No. 104-67, 109 Stat 737 (Dec. 22, 1995).

> No covered class action based upon the statutory or common law of any State . . . may be maintained in any State or Federal court by any private party alleging—
>
> > (1) an untrue statement or omission of a material fact in connection with the purchase or sale of a covered security; or
> >
> > (2) that the defendant used or employed any manipulative or deceptive device or contrivance in connection with the purchase or sale of a covered security.[200]

In addition, as an additional protection in case state courts refused to dismiss state-law class action claims as required by SLUSA, SLUSA provided defendants a removal right.[201]

In *Cyan*, the Supreme Court considered whether SLUSA applies, not only to state-law securities class actions, but also to class actions asserting Securities Act claims in state court, such that the actions are subject to dismissal or, at the very least, subject to removal. Based on an interpretation of the text of SLUSA, which by its terms applies only to covered class actions "based upon the statutory or common law of any State," Supreme Court answered both of these questions in the negative: "SLUSA did nothing to strip state courts of their longstanding jurisdiction to adjudicate class actions alleging only 1933 Act violations. Neither did SLUSA authorize removing such suits from state to federal court."[202]

When reaching this conclusion, the Court acknowledged that SLUSA added a confusing "except" clause to the Securities Act's grant of concurrent jurisdiction to federal and state courts:

> The district courts of the United States . . . shall have jurisdiction concurrent with State and Territorial courts, *except as provided in section 77p of this title with respect to covered class actions*, of all suits in equity and actions at law brought to enforce any liability or duty created by this subchapter.[203]

The Court acknowledged that, since Securities Act claims are not covered class actions to which section 77p applies, this except clause is a non-sequitur: "[I]t would be as if a parent told her child 'you may have fruit after dinner, except for lollipops.'"[204] Although the Court was unsure why Congress inserted this except clause into the Securities Act's grant of concurrent jurisdiction, the Court postulated that it might be an example of hyper-vigilance: "The idea, to return to our prior example, is to make sure that even if the child thinks orange lollipops count as fruit, she will not act

---

200. 15 U.S.C. §§ 77p(b) & 78bb(f)(1).
201. 15 U.S.C. §§ 77p(c) & 78bb(f)(2).
202. *Cyan*, 138 S. Ct. at 1078.
203. 15 U.S.C. § 77v(a) (emphasis added).
204. *Cyan*, 138 S. Ct. at 1073.

on that view."[205] Regardless, the Court declined to interpret the oddity of the except clause "to devise a statute (and at that, a transformative one) of our own."[206]

Post-*Cyan*, when Securities Act class actions are asserted in state court, the PSLRA's substantive restrictions will continue to apply, while its procedural restrictions will not. For example, the *Cyan* Court cited the PSLRA's sworn-certification requirement for lead plaintiffs as a procedural requirement that will not apply in state court and the PSLRA's safe harbor for forward-looking statements as a substantive provision that will apply in state court.[207] As commentators have discussed, the applicability in state court of other PSLRA provisions, such as the discovery stay, will likely be hotly litigated.[208] In addition, plaintiffs' ability to evade the PSLRA's procedural restrictions by filing in state court may lead to an influx of Securities Act class actions in state court, the potential for forum-shopping among state jurisdictions, and the potential for parallel litigation.

In response, as some issuers have already done,[209] issuers may seek to include an exclusive-venue provision in their articles of incorporation or bylaws. For example, the following sample exclusive-venue provision has been widely attributed to Professor Joseph Grundfest[210]:

> Unless the Corporation consents in writing to the selection of an alternative forum, the federal district courts of the United States of America shall be the exclusive forum for the resolution of any complaint asserting a cause of action arising under the Securities Act of 1933. Any person or entity purchasing or otherwise acquiring any interest in any security of the Corporation shall be deemed to have notice of and consented to this provision.

The validity of such exclusive-venue provisions under state corporate law is already being litigated.[211]

---

205. *Id.* at 1074.

206. *Id.* at 1075.

207. *Id.* at 1072.

208. *E.g.*, Israel David & Samuel P. Groner, *State Court Securities Lawsuits and the PSLRA in a Post-'Cyan' Era*, N.Y.L.J. (May 2, 2018), at https://www.law.com/newyorklawjournal/2018/05/02/state-court-securities-lawsuits-and-the-pslra-in-a-post-cyan-era/ (last visited Oct. 12, 2018) (arguing that the PSLRA's discovery stay and sanctions for abusive litigation should apply in state court).

209. Jacob Rund, *More IPO Companies Are Pushing Securities Suits to Federal Court*, BLOOMBERG LAW (May 14, 2018), at https://www.bna.com/ipo-companies-pushing-n73014475899/ (last visited Oct. 12, 2018).

210. *E.g.*, Verified Class Action Complaint for Declaratory Judgment, Sciabacucchi v. Salzberg, Case No. 2018-931, 2017 WL 6815531, at para. 46 (Del. Ch.) (filed Dec. 29, 2017) (citing Professor Joseph Grundfest's May 6, 2016 presentation at the Rock Center for Corporate Governance as the genesis of this provision).

211. *E.g.*, *id.* at 1 ("Plaintiff seeks a judgment declaring invalid a provision included in each of the Companies' respective certificates of incorporation, purporting to require any claim under the Securities Act of 1933 . . . to be brought in federal court.").

B. Class Action Tolling

In the recent decision of *China Agritech, Inc. v. Resh*, the Supreme Court held that *American Pipe* tolling of statutes of limitations does not apply to successive class actions.[212]

As background, securities claims are subject to both statutes of limitations and statutes of repose. For example, § 11 claims are subject to a one-year statute of limitations and a three-year statute of repose,[213] while § 10(b) claims are subject to a two-year statute of limitations and a five-year statute of repose.[214]

In *American Pipe & Construction Co. v. Utah*, the Supreme Court held that the filing of a putative class action tolls the running of the statute of limitations "for all purported members of the class who make timely motions to intervene after the court has found the suit inappropriate for class action status."[215] In *Crown, Cork & Seal Co. v. Parker*, the Court extended that tolling to class members who, rather than filing motions to intervene, file separate actions.[216] In *California Public Employees' Retirement System v. ANZ Securities, Inc.*, the Court clarified that class action tolling is grounded in equity[217] and that, as such, it applies only to statutes of limitations, not to statutes of repose.[218] Thus, although class action tolling applies to § 11's one-year statute of limitations and § 10(b)'s two-year statute of limitations, it does not apply to § 11's three-year statute of repose or § 10(b)'s five-year statute of repose.

In *China Agritech*, the Court addressed whether class action tolling tolls the statute of limitations only for later-filed individual actions, or whether it also applies to later-filed class actions. Citing the goals of efficiency and economy, the Court limited the applicability of class action tolling to later-filed individual actions:

> We hold that *American Pipe* does not permit a plaintiff who waits out the statute of limitations to piggyback on an earlier, timely filed class action. The "efficiency and economy of litigation" that support tolling of individual claims do not support maintenance of untimely successive class actions; any additional *class* filings should be made early on, soon after the commencement of the first action seeking class certification.

---

212. China Agritech, Inc. v. Resh, 138 S. Ct. 1800 (2018).
213. 15 U.S.C. § 77m; Cal. Public Employees' Ret. Sys. v. ANZ Secs., 137 S. Ct. 2042, 2049-50 (2017) (classifying the one-year period as a statute of limitations and the three-year period as a statute of repose).
214. 28 U.S.C. § 1658(b); *China Agritech*, 138 S. Ct. at 1804 (classifying the two-year period as a statute of limitations and the five-year period as a statute of repose).
215. Am. Pipe & Constr. Co. v. Utah, 414 U.S. 538, 553 (1974).
216. Crown, Cork & Seal Co. v. Parker, 462 U.S. 345, 350 (1983).
217. *ANZ Securities*, 137 S. Ct. at 2051-52.
218. *Id.* at 2052.

American Pipe tolls the limitation period for individual claims because economy of litigation favors delaying those claims until after a class-certification denial. If certification is granted, the claims will proceed as a class and there would be no need for the assertion of any claim individually. If certification is denied, only then would it be necessary to pursue claims individually.

With class claims, on the other hand, efficiency favors early assertion of competing class representative claims.[219]

Otherwise, the statute of limitations could be "extended time and again; as each class is denied certification, a new named plaintiff could file a class complaint that resuscitates the litigation."[220] The Court concluded that "[e]ndless tolling of a statute of limitations is not a result envisioned by *American Pipe*."[221]

Post-*China Agritech*, if class certification is denied, it is still possible for a new plaintiff to assert a successive securities class action, but that action must be filed, not only within the applicable statute of repose, but also within the applicable statute of limitations—without reliance on class action tolling. As one commentator noted, "it remains to be seen whether the decision will precipitate more 'protective' class action filings" within the statute of limitations, just in case class certification is denied in a pending class action.[222] Another commentator predicted: "[T]he impact of *China Agritech* is modest in practice because most class action lawyers have incentives to file copycat class actions soon after the first case is filed in order to try to secure lead counsel status."[223]

C.   Mandatory Arbitration of Securities Claims

The potential for issuers to include provisions that mandate arbitration of securities claims in their charters or bylaws has generated significant debate over the past year. As summarized by Claudia H. Allen, until recently, the

---

219. *China Agritech*, 138 S. Ct. at 1806-07 (internal citations omitted).

220. *Id.* at 1808.

221. *Id.* at 1809.

222. Aphrodite Kokolis, *U.S. Supreme Court Rejects Tolling of Limitations Periods in Successive Class Actions*, NAT'L L.J. (June 18, 2018), at https://www.natlawreview.com/article/us-supreme-court-rejects-tolling-limitations-periods-successive-class-actions (last visited Oct. 13, 2018).

223. Archis A. Parasharami, *Supreme Court Holds in* China Agritech *That American Pipe's Equitable Tolling Rule Does Not Extend to Successive Class Actions*, MAYER BROWN CLASS DEFENSE BLOG (June 11, 2018), at https://www.classdefenseblog.com/2018/06/supreme-court-holds-in-china-agritech-that-american-pipes-equitable-tolling-rule-does-not-extend-to-successive-class-actions/ (last visited Oct. 13, 2018).

SEC staff viewed these provisions as contrary to the anti-waiver provisions of § 14 of the Securities Act[224] and § 29(a) of the Exchange Act[225]:

> The Staff's position was illustrated most recently in 2012, when The Carlyle Group L.P. sought to go public with a mandatory arbitration provision in its limited partnership agreement. Consistent with its historical position, the Staff stated that it did not anticipate exercising its authority to accelerate the effective date of the company's registration statement if the limited partnership agreement included such a provision, adding, "the Commission would need to make any decision on a request for acceleration." The company eliminated the arbitration provision seemingly as a result of the Staff's position and significant negative publicity, and substituted a different type of forum selection provision–namely, an exclusive forum clause. . . .

> The Staff's position was also evident during the 2012 proxy season when Gannett Co., Inc. and Pfizer Inc. each received a binding stockholder proposal to adopt a bylaw requiring arbitration of stockholder disputes, subject to specified parameters. Each company sought SEC no-action relief under Exchange Act Rule 14a-8 ("Shareholder Proposals"), arguing that the proposal, if implemented, would cause the company to violate the anti-waiver provision in Section 29(a) of the Exchange Act. The Staff granted no-action relief without being explicit about the basis of the decision, stating, "We note that there appears to be some basis for your view that implementation of the proposal would cause the company to violate the federal securities laws."[226]

But, the debate was re-opened in July 2017 in a speech by then-SEC Commissioner Michael Piwowar: "For shareholder lawsuits, companies can come to us to ask for relief to put mandatory arbitration into their charters. I would encourage companies to come and talk to us about that."[227]

Since then, various scholars, regulators, and interested parties have weighed in.[228] For example, in October 2017, the Department of the Treasury issued a report to President Trump on "A Financial System That

---

224. 15 U.S.C. § 77n ("Any condition, stipulation, or provision binding any person acquiring any security to waive compliance with any provision of this Act or of the rules and regulations of the Commission shall be void.")

225. 15 U.S.C. § 78cc(a) ("Any condition, stipulation, or provision binding any person to waive compliance with any provision of this Act or of any rule or regulation thereunder, or of any rule of a self-regulatory organization, shall be void.").

226. Claudia H. Allen, *Bylaws Mandating Arbitration of Stockholder Disputes?*, 39 DEL. J. CORP. L. 751, 778-79 (2015) (citations omitted).

227. Sarah N. Lynch, *U.S. SEC's Piwowar Urgers Companies to Pursue Mandatory Arbitration Clauses*, REUTERS (July 17, 2017), at https://www.reuters.com/article/us-usa-sec-arbitration-idUSKBN1A221Y (last visited Oct. 14, 2018).

228. For a comprehensive summary, see Kevin M. LaCroix, *Mandatory Arbitration of Shareholder Claims: What's the Latest?*, THE D&O DIARY (April 29, 2018), at https://www.dandodiary.com/2018/04/articles/securities-laws/mandatory-arbitration-shareholder-claims-whats-latest/ (last visited Oct. 14, 2018).

Creates Economic Opportunities: Capital Markets."[229] The report identifies fewer public companies and IPOs as an issue, cites concerns about class action litigation as a potential factor, and recommends exploring mandatory arbitration as a solution:

> The potential for class action securities litigation may discourage companies from listing their shares on public markets and encourage companies that are already public to "go private" rather than face the cost and uncertainty of securities litigation. . . .
>
> Treasury recommends that the states and the SEC continue to investigate the various means to reduce costs of securities litigation for issuers in a way that protects investors' rights and interests, including allowing companies and shareholders to settle disputes through arbitration.[230]

Professor Stephen Bainbridge agrees, arguing that mandatory arbitration of shareholder class action lawsuits is "an idea whose time has come":

> In contrast to federal litigation, securities arbitration appears to provide a more efficient and cost-effective mechanism to resolve disputes with integrity while minimizing the burdens on our judicial system. Arbitration ensures that all relevant facts are presented to the panel without the evidentiary hurdles of federal court. In addition, the use of arbitrators knowledgeable about the securities industry may reduce the uncertainty of resolving securities claims in jury trials.[231]

One voice on the other side is that of Rick Fleming, the SEC Investor Advocate. In a February 2018 speech, he cited "the importance of private suits in helping to protect investors and deter wrongdoing," the importance of a class-wide remedy in order to provide "recourse for investors with small holdings," and the hindering of "the evolution of case law" if mandatory arbitration were widespread.[232]

Similarly, in a July 2018 letter to Chairman Jay Clayton, the State Treasurers of six states expressed their opposition to forced arbitration or class action waivers:

---

229. U.S. Department of the Treasury, A Financial System That Creates Economic Opportunities: Capital Markets (Oct. 2017), at https://www.treasury.gov/press-center/press-releases/Documents/A-Financial-System-Capital-Markets-FINAL-FINAL.pdf (last visited Oct. 14, 2018).

230. *Id.* at 34-35.

231. Stephen Bainbridge, *The SEC Should Authorize Mandatory Arbitration of Shareholder Class Action Lawsuits*, PROFESSORBAINBRIDGE.COM (Jan. 30, 2018), at http://www.professorbainbridge.com/professorbainbridgecom/2018/01/the-sec-should-authorize-mandatory-arbitration-of-shareholder-class-action-lawsuits.html (last visited Oct. 14, 2018).

232. Rick Fleming, SEC Investor Advocate, Speech, Mandatory Arbitration: An Illusory Remedy for Public Company Shareholders (Feb. 24, 2018), at https://www.sec.gov/news/speech/fleming-sec-speaks-mandatory-arbitration (last visited Oct. 14, 2018).

Private savings can enhance quality of life and increase opportunities for the citizens of the states we serve, and private savings can also reduce the need for state resources and public assistance. Targeted, private enforcement of state and federal securities laws furthers these goals by empowering Americans to directly combat financial misconduct, and get back their hard-earned investment dollars.

Forced arbitration provisions and class action waivers do just the opposite. . . . Unfortunately, individual police and firefighter pensioners, teachers and municipal workers, and other individual and retail investors simply do not possess the financial size or scale to contest the inclusion of a forced arbitration clause or class action waiver in a company charter or corporate bylaw. The choice is either to forego any reasonable hope of accountability in the wake of securities fraud, or to forego the investment entirely. We can all support concepts of individual choice and freedom of contract without sacrificing our commitment to ensure that such investment choices and contractual relationships are informed and not predatory.

Moreover, forced arbitration, by its very nature, helps to keep corporate misconduct and financial fraud secret by preventing such cases from reaching the light of public U.S. courtrooms.[233]

Finally, in an April 24, 2018 letter to Representative Carolyn B. Maloney, Chairman Jay Clayton stated that he has "not formed a definitive view on whether or not mandatory arbitration for shareholder disputes is appropriate in the context of an IPO for a U.S. Company" and that "this issue is not a priority" for him.[234] He further stated that, if the issue were to be presented to the SEC, he "would expect that any decision would involve Commission action (and not be made through delegated authority) and that the Commission would give the issue full consideration in a measured and deliberate manner."[235] Chairman Clayton also cited the 2013 Supreme Court decision in *American Express Co. v. Italian Colors Restaurant*, in which the Court reiterated that courts must "rigorously enforce" arbitration agreements unless the Federal Arbitration Act's mandate has been "overridden by a contrary congressional command,"[236] and noted that "commentators have

---

233. States Treasurers' Opposition Against Forced Arbitration or Class Action Waivers in Shareholder Agreements, Harvard Law School Forum on Corporate Governance and Financial Regulation (July 13, 2018), at https://corpgov.law.harvard.edu/2018/07/13/state-treasurers-opposition-against-forced-arbitration-or-class-action-waivers-in-shareholder-agreements/ (last visited Oct. 14, 2018).
234. Letter from SEC Chairman Jay Clayton to Representative Carolyn B. Maloney, at 2 (April 24, 2018), at https://maloney.house.gov/sites/maloney.house.gov/files/MALONEY%20ET%20AL%20-%20FORCED%20ARBITRATION%20-%20ES156546%20Response.pdf (last visited Oct. 14, 2018).
235. *Id.*
236. American Express Co. v. Italian Colors Restaurant, 570 U.S. 228, 233 (2013).

observed that there is uncertainty as to whether the Commission would have a basis to deny an acceleration request in these circumstances."[237]

Against this backdrop, the following prediction from Kevin M. LaCroix is apt:

> Under these circumstances, a prospective IPO company candidate might well choose to include within its pre-effective registration statement submission incorporating a corporate charter with a mandatory arbitration provision, if for no other reason than to try to force a decision on the issue. Indeed a company could try this at any time.
>
> For that reason, it seems unlikely to me that this issue is just going to go away, even though it is not a priority for Clayton. To the contrary, it seems likelier to me that this issue is going to bubble up and require Commission action, sooner rather than later.[238]

VIII.   Securities and Exchange Commission Enforcement

The Securities and Exchange Commission is charged with enforcing the securities laws, and the past year has seen renewed scrutiny of SEC administrative proceedings, including the appointment and removal of SEC administrative law judges. In addition, the protections and incentives for whistleblowers have been reduced, with the Supreme Court's limiting the scope of Dodd-Frank's anti-retaliation protections for whistleblowers and the SEC's proposing new potential reductions to whistleblower awards.

A.   Administrative Proceedings

The SEC can elect to pursue securities laws violators by asserting civil enforcement actions in federal court or by instituting administrative proceedings. The Dodd-Frank Act expanded the SEC's authority to impose civil penalties on non-regulated entities in administrative proceedings.[239] Not surprisingly, "[i]n the years following Dodd-Frank, the SEC began con-

237. Letter from SEC Chairman Jay Clayton to Representative Carolyn B. Maloney, at 5-6 (April 24, 2018), at https://maloney.house.gov/sites/maloney.house.gov/files/MALONEY%20ET%20AL%20-%20FORCED%20ARBITRATION%20-%20ES156546%20Response.pdf (last visited Oct. 14, 2018).

238. Kevin M. LaCroix, *Mandatory Arbitration of Shareholder Claims: What's the Latest?*, THE D&O DIARY (April 29, 2018), at https://www.dandodiary.com/2018/04/articles/securities-laws/mandatory-arbitration-shareholder-claims-whats-latest/ (last visited Oct. 14, 2018).

239. Dodd-Frank Wall Street Reform and Consumer Protection Act of 2012, Pub. L. No. 111-203, § 929P, 124 Stat 1376 (July 21, 2010).

sistently increasing the amount of cases it brought against non-regulated entities through administrative proceedings."[240] In a recently published empirical study, Professors Stephen J. Choi and A.C. Pritchard made the following findings about SEC enforcement post-Dodd-Frank:

> Our empirical results show a decline in the number of court actions and an increase in the number of administrative proceedings post-Dodd-Frank. We also show an increase in average civil penalties post-Dodd-Frank for both court actions and administrative proceedings. We also show greater cooperation by companies with the SEC in connection with its enforcement actions.
>
> Cases brought in administrative proceedings have become more complex post-Dodd-Frank. We show an increase in the disgorgement amount and the number of years during which the violation allegedly took place. At the same time, administrative proceedings following Dodd-Frank tended to be weaker (i.e., less likely to prevail) and less salient (i.e., less likely to garner media attention). These findings are consistent with the SEC attempting to maximize the monetary penalties it imposes as well as positive media attention from its enforcement actions, while allocating its limited resources between administrative proceedings and civil court actions in a cost-effective way.[241]

Against this backdrop, the power of the SEC's administrative law judges ("ALJs") has been subject to increased scrutiny. The Supreme Court recently summarized the power of the SEC's ALJs:

> The SEC has statutory authority to enforce the nation's securities laws. One way it can do so is by instituting an administrative proceeding against an alleged wrongdoer. By law, the Commission may itself preside over such a proceeding. See 17 C.F.R. § 201.110 (2017). But the Commission also may, and typically does, delegate that task to an ALJ. See *ibid.*; 15 U.S.C. § 78d-1(a). The SEC currently has five ALJs. . . .
>
> An ALJ assigned to hear an SEC enforcement action has extensive powers— the "authority to do all things necessary and appropriate to discharge his or her duties" and ensure a "fair and orderly" adversarial proceeding. §§ 201.111, 200.14(a). Those powers "include, but are not limited to," supervising discovery; issuing, revoking, or modifying subpoenas; deciding motions; ruling on the admissibility of evidence; administering oaths; hearing and examining witnesses; generally "[r]egulating the course of" the proceeding and the "conduct of the parties and their counsel"; and imposing sanctions for "[c]ontemptuous conduct" or violations of procedural requirements. §§ 201.111, 201.180; see §§ 200.14(a), 201.230. As that list suggests, an SEC

---

240. Ryan Jones, *The Fight over Home Court: An Analysis of the SEC's Increased Use of Administrative Proceedings*, 68 SMU L. Rev. 507, 517 (2015).

241. Stephen J. Choi & A.C. Pritchard, *The SEC's Shift to Administrative Proceedings: An Empirical Assessment*, 34 Yale J. on Reg. 1, 4 (2017).

ALJ exercises authority "comparable to" that of a federal district judge conducting a bench trial. *Butz v. Economou,* 438 U.S. 478, 513 (1978).

After a hearing ends, the ALJ issues an "initial decision." § 201.360(a)(1). That decision must set out "findings and conclusions" about all "material issues of fact [and] law"; it also must include the "appropriate order, sanction, relief, or denial thereof." § 201.360(b). The Commission can then review the ALJ's decision, either upon request or *sua sponte.* See § 201.360(d)(1). But if it opts against review, the Commission "issue[s] an order that the [ALJ's] decision has become final." § 201.360(d)(2). At that point, the initial decision is "deemed the action of the Commission." § 78d-1(c).[242]

In particular, parties have challenged (1) the appointment of the SEC's ALJs by SEC staff and (2) statutory restrictions on the removal of the SEC's ALJs.

1.   *Appointment of Administrative Law Judges*

In the recent decision of *Lucia v. SEC,* the Supreme Court held that the SEC's ALJs are inferior "Officers of the United States" as opposed to non-officer employees and that, as a consequence, they must be appointed pursuant to the Appointments Clause.[243] In order to reach this conclusion, the Court applied the "significant authority" test from *Buckley v. Valeo,*[244] drawing guidance from how that test was applied in *Freytag v. Commissioner,* in which the Court held that Tax Court special trial judges (STJs) are officers.[245] According to the Court, STJs are "near-carbon copies of the Commission's ALJs":[246]

> *Freytag* says everything necessary to decide this case. To begin, the Commission's ALJs, like the Tax Court's STJs, hold a continuing office established by law. . . . Far from serving temporarily or episodically, SEC ALJs "receive[ ] a career appointment." And that appointment is to a position created by statute, down to its "duties, salary, and means of appointment."

> Still more, the Commission's ALJs exercise the same "significant discretion" when carrying out the same "important functions" as STJs do. Both sets of officials have all the authority needed to ensure fair and orderly adversarial hearings—indeed, nearly all the tools of federal trial judges. Consider in order the four specific (if overlapping) powers *Freytag* mentioned. First, the Commission's ALJs (like the Tax Court's STJs) "take testimony." More precisely, they "[r]eceiv[e] evidence" and "[e]xamine witnesses" at hearings, and

---

242. Lucia v. SEC, 138 S. Ct. 2044, 2049 (2018) (some citations shortened).
243. *Lucia,* 138 S. Ct. 2044.
244. Buckley v. Valeo, 424 U.S. 1, 126 (1976).
245. Freytag v. Commissioner, 501 U.S. 868 (1991).
246. *Lucia,* 138 S. Ct. at 2052.

may also take pre-hearing depositions. Second, the ALJs (like STJs) "conduct trials." As detailed earlier, they administer oaths, rule on motions, and generally "regulat[e] the course of" a hearing, as well as the conduct of parties and counsel. Third, the ALJs (like STJs) "rule on the admissibility of evidence." They thus critically shape the administrative record (as they also do when issuing document subpoenas). And fourth, the ALJs (like STJs) "have the power to enforce compliance with discovery orders." In particular, they may punish all "[c]ontemptuous conduct," including violations of those orders, by means as severe as excluding the offender from the hearing. So point for point—straight from *Freytag*'s list—the Commission's ALJs have equivalent duties and powers as STJs in conducting adversarial inquiries.

And at the close of those proceedings, ALJs issue decisions much like that in *Freytag*—except with potentially more independent effect. As the *Freytag* Court recounted, STJs "prepare proposed findings and an opinion" adjudicating charges and assessing tax liabilities. Similarly, the Commission's ALJs issue decisions containing factual findings, legal conclusions, and appropriate remedies. And what happens next reveals that the ALJ can play the more autonomous role. In a major case like *Freytag*, a regular Tax Court judge must always review an STJ's opinion. And that opinion counts for nothing unless the regular judge adopts it as his own. By contrast, the SEC can decide against reviewing an ALJ decision at all. And when the SEC declines review (and issues an order saying so), the ALJ's decision itself "becomes final" and is "deemed the action of the Commission." That last-word capacity makes this an a fortiori case: If the Tax Court's STJs are officers, as *Freytag* held, then the Commission's ALJs must be too.[247]

Therefore, because the SEC's ALJs are inferior officers, they must be appointed pursuant to the Appointments Clause, which requires appointment by the President, a court of law, or a head of department.[248] The SEC's ALJs were appointed by SEC staff, not by the Commission itself, and thus their appointment violated the Appointments Clause. The Supreme Court reversed the Court of Appeals' judgment affirming the ALJ's decision and remanded, with instructions for the administrative proceeding to be reheard by the SEC itself or by a properly appointed ALJ (other than the one who heard the initial case).[249]

While *Lucia* was pending, the SEC sought to preemptively cure the Constitutional defect in the appointment of its ALJs by issuing an order ratifying the prior appointments of its ALJs.[250] After *Lucia* was decided, the SEC reiterated those appointments: "In an abundance of caution and for avoidance of doubt, we today reiterate our approval of their appointments

247. *Id.* at 2053-54 (internal citations omitted).
248. Const. art. II, § 2.
249. *Lucia,* 138 S. Ct. at 2055.
250. Order, In re: Pending Administrative Proceedings, SEC Release No. 4816 (Nov. 30, 2017).

as our own under the Constitution."[251] In addition, with respect to any proceeding currently pending before an ALJ or the SEC, the SEC sought to cure any Constitutional defect by providing "the opportunity for a new hearing before an ALJ who did not previously participate in the matter."[252]

2.   Removal of Administrative Law Judges

In its certiorari-stage briefing and in its merits briefing in *Lucia*, the Government asked the Supreme Court to address a second question: "whether the statutory restrictions on removing the Commission's ALJs are constitutional."[253] The *Lucia* Court declined to address this question because no lower court had yet addressed it.[254] This issue remains unsettled.

The SEC's ALJs, who, per *Lucia*, are inferior officers, are subject to two levels of protection from removal without cause. First, the Merits Systems Protection Board can remove the ALJs only "for good cause."[255] Second, the members of the Merits Systems Protection Board, who are appointed to seven-year terms, may be removed by the President only for "inefficiency, neglect of duty, or malfeasance in office."[256]

In the wake of the Supreme Court's decision in *Free Entreprise Fund v. Public Company Accounting Oversight Board*,[257] it is possible that the two levels of protection from removal without cause afforded to the SEC's ALJs contravene the Constitution's separation of powers. As a reminder, in *Free Enterprise Fund*, the Court analyzed whether the following dual for-cause removal protections afforded to the members of the Public Company Accounting Oversight Board ("PCAOB") were unconstitutional: (1) the SEC could remove the members of the PCAOB only "for good cause shown," and (2) the President could remove the members of the SEC only for "inefficiency, neglect of duty, or malfeasance in office."[258] The Court held that "such multilevel protection from removal is contrary to Article II's vesting of the executive power in the President."[259] The two layers of protection from removal without cause deemed unconstitutional in *Free Enterprise Fund* are strikingly similar to those afforded to the SEC's ALJs, suggesting that the ALJ removal protections likewise might be unconstitutional. Indeed,

---

251. Order, In re: Pending Administrative Proceedings, SEC Release No. 10536 (Aug. 22, 2018).

252. *Id.*

253. *Lucia*, 138 S. Ct. at 2049 n.1.

254. *Id.*

255. 5 U.S.C. § 7521(a).

256. 5 U.S.C. § 1202(d).

257. Free Enterprise Fund v. Public Company Accounting Oversight Board, 561 U.S. 477 (2010).

258. *Id.* at 486-87.

259. *Id.* at 484.

in his *Lucia* opinion concurring in the judgment in part and dissenting in part, Justice Breyer recognized this possibility:

> *If* the *Free Enterprise Fund*'s holding applies equally to the administrative law judges—and I stress the "if"—then to hold that the administrative law judges are "Officers of the United States" is, *perhaps*, to hold that their removal protections are unconstitutional. This would risk transforming administrative law judges from independent adjudicators into *dependent* decisionmakers, serving at the pleasure of the Commission. . . .
>
> I have stressed the words "if" and "perhaps" in the previous paragraph because *Free Enterprise Fund*'s holding may not invalidate the removal protections applicable to the Commission's administrative law judges even if the judges are inferior "officers of the United States" for purposes of the Appointments Clause.[260]

Professor Alan Morrison has suggested that it may be difficult for a party to obtain standing to raise a constitutional challenge to the SEC's ALJ's dual protection from removal without cause:

> One additional possibility exists to avoid the removal problem, despite *Free Enterprise*. If the president ordered the removal of an ALJ, the issue would be properly presented and no one would suggest that an ALJ did not have standing to object to the removal. But because the power of removal is intended to protect the president and enable him to carry out his duties, it is questionable whether the party who lost before an ALJ (and the agency) has standing to object that the president might not have been able to fire the ALJ if he had been so inclined. To be sure, *Free Enterprise* allowed a regulated party to make the removal objection (although in that case it was part of an appointment objection on which there could be no standing issue). But if the court were to follow its strict approach to standing (see most recently Gill v. Whitford[, 138 S. Ct. 1916 (2018)]) that might be a way to postpone, if not avoid entirely, facing the removal question. And for those like me and the 28 law professors whom I joined as amici in this case, the protections against at-will removal applicable to ALJs are vital safeguards for regulated parties—including the petitioners in this case.[261]

---

260. *Lucia*, 138 S. Ct. at 2060 (Breyer, J., concurring in the judgment in part and dissenting in part).

261. Alan Morrison, *Symposium: Lucia v. SEC—more questions than answers*, SCOTUSBLOG (June 22, 2018), http://www.scotusblog.com/2018/06/symposium-lucia-v-sec-more-questions-than-answers/ (last visited Oct. 13, 2018).

B. Whistleblowers

The Dodd-Frank Act included two new whistleblower provisions meant to "work synchronously to motivate individuals with knowledge of illegal activity to 'tell the SEC'"[262]: (1) an anti-retaliation provision; and (2) a whistleblower award program. Each provision has been the subject of recent action.

1. Protection from Retaliation

The Dodd-Frank Act added the following three-pronged provision prohibiting retaliation against whistleblowers:

> No employer may discharge, demote, suspend, threaten, harass, directly or indirectly, or in any other manner discriminate against, a whistleblower in the terms and conditions of employment because of any lawful act done by the whistleblower—
>
> > (i) in providing information to the Commission in accordance with this section;
> >
> > (ii) in initiating, testifying in, or assisting in any investigation or judicial or administrative action of the Commission based upon or related to such information; or
> >
> > (iii) in making disclosures that are required or protected under the Sarbanes-Oxley Act of 2002 (15 U.S.C. 7201 et seq.), this chapter, including section 78j-1(m) of this title, section 1513(e) of Title 18, and any other law, rule, or regulation subject to the jurisdiction of the Commission.[263]

In addition, the Act defined "whistleblower" as follows: "The term 'whistleblower' means any individual who provides, or 2 or more individuals acting jointly who provide, information relating to a violation of the securities laws to the Commission, in a manner established, by rule or regulation, by the Commission."[264]

When implementing Dodd-Frank's anti-retaliation provision, the SEC issued Rule 21F-2, defining "whistleblower" for purposes of the anti-retaliation provision as follows:

> For purposes of the anti-retaliation protections afforded by Section 21F(h)(1) of the Exchange Act (15 U.S.C. 78u-6(h)(1)), you are a whistleblower if:

---

262. Digital Realty Trust, Inc. v. Somers, 138 S. Ct. 767, 778 (2018).
263. 15 U.S.C. § 78u-6(h)(1)(A).
264. 15 U.S.C. § 78u-6(a)(6).

(i) You possess a reasonable belief that the information you are providing relates to a possible securities law violation (or, where applicable, to a possible violation of the provisions set forth in 18 U.S.C. 1514A(a)) that has occurred, is ongoing, or is about to occur, and;

(ii) You provide that information in a manner described in Section 21F(h)(1)(A) of the Exchange Act (15 U.S.C. 78u-6(h)(1)(A)).

(iii) The anti-retaliation protections apply whether or not you satisfy the requirements, procedures and conditions to qualify for an award.

In other words, Rule 21F-2 included within the definition of "whistle-blower" anyone who acted within the scope of the above-quoted three-pronged anti-retaliation provision, even though the third prong does not require the person to provide information to the SEC.

In the recent case of *Digital Realty Trust, Inc. v. Somers*, the Supreme Court held that the SEC had exceeded its statutory authority when adopting Rule 21F-2 because the rule expanded the scope of "whistleblower" to include those who report information to someone other than the SEC:

Does the anti-retaliation provision of Dodd-Frank extend to an individual who has not reported a violation of the securities laws to the SEC and therefore falls outside the Act's definition of "whistleblower"? We answer that question "No": To sue under Dodd-Frank's anti-retaliation provision, a person must first "provid[e] . . . information relating to a violation of the securities laws to the Commission."[265]

The Court rejected the argument that limiting the definition of "whistle-blower" to those who provide information to the SEC would eviscerate the third prong of the anti-retaliation provision:

With the statutory definition incorporated, clause (iii) protects a whistle-blower who reports misconduct both to the SEC and to another entity, but suffers retaliation because of the latter, non-SEC, disclosure. That would be so, for example, where the retaliating employer is unaware that the employee has alerted the SEC. In such a case, without clause (iii), retaliation for internal reporting would not be reached by Dodd-Frank, for clause (i) applies only where the employer retaliates against the employee "because of" the SEC reporting. § 78u-6(h)(1)(A). Moreover, even where the employer knows of the SEC reporting, the third clause may operate to dispel a proof problem: The employee can recover under the statute without having to demonstrate whether the retaliation was motivated by the internal report (thus yielding protection under clause (iii)) or by the SEC disclosure (thus gaining protection under clause (i)).[266]

---

265. *Digital Realty*, 138 S. Ct. at 772-73.
266. *Id.* at 779.

Therefore, post-*Digital Realty*, internal whistleblowers are not protected by Dodd-Frank's anti-retaliation provision unless they also report to the SEC. Of note, certain internal whistleblowers are protected by the anti-retaliation provision in the Sarbanes-Oxley Act.[267] However, Sarbanes-Oxley's anti-retaliation provision "contains an administrative-exhaustion requirement, a 180-day administrative complaint-filing deadline, and a remedial scheme limited to actual damages," while the Dodd-Frank anti-retaliation provision "provides for immediate access to federal court, a generous statute of limitations (at least six years), and the opportunity to recover double backpay."[268] The Supreme Court acknowledged that auditors and attorneys are subject to internal-reporting requirements and that there is the potential for them to "face retaliation quickly, before they have a chance to report to the SEC."[269] In that circumstance, the auditors and attorneys would not be able to assert claims under Dodd-Frank's anti-retaliation provision. The Court postulated, however, that "Congress may well have considered adequate the safeguards already afforded by Sarbanes-Oxley, protections specifically designed to shield lawyers, accountants, and similar professionals."[270]

2.   *Whistleblower Awards*

The Dodd-Frank Act also created a whistleblower award program,[271] which is administered by the SEC's Office of the Whistleblower. In 2011, the SEC adopted a comprehensive set of rules to implement the whistleblower program.[272] In 2018, the SEC awarded its three highest-ever whistleblower awards since the program has been in effect: $50 million on March 19, 2018; $39 million on September 6, 2018; and $33 million on March 19, 2018.[273]

On June 29, 2018, the SEC proposed several rule amendments to the whistleblower program.[274] The most controversial is a proposed amendment to add "additional considerations in connection with certain large awards where the monetary sanctions would equal or exceed $100 million."[275] As proposed, the SEC could reduce such an award, subject to a floor of $30 million, to an amount "reasonably necessary to reward the whistleblower

267. 18 U.S.C. § 1514.

268. *Digital Realty*, 138 S. Ct. at 778.

269. *Id.* at 780.

270. *Id.*

271. 15 U.S.C. § 78u-6.

272. 17 C.F.R. §§ 240.21F-1-240.21F-17.

273. SEC Whistleblower Program Info & Statistics ("Top 10 Awards"), at https://www.sec.gov/page/whistleblower-100million (last visited Oct. 13, 2018).

274. Amendments to the Commissions Whistleblower Program Rules, SEC Release No. 34-83557 (June 29, 2018).

275. *Id.* at 170 (proposing a new paragraph (3) to Rule 21F-6(b)(2)).

and to incentivize similarly situated whistleblowers."[276] In the proposing release, the SEC explained this proposed amendment as follows:

> An important principle underlying proposed paragraph (d) is that, as the dollar value of an award amount grows exceedingly large, there is a significant potential for a diminishing marginal benefit to the program in terms of compensating the whistleblower and incentivizing future whistleblowers. In these situations, we believe that it is in the public interest that we scrutinize the dollar impact of these awards more carefully in considering award enhancements and reductions under the existing award criteria of paragraphs (a) and (b) of this section and, further, where appropriate, adjust an award downward so that the dollar amount of the payout is more in line with the program's goals of rewarding whistleblowers and incentivizing future whistleblowers from a cost-benefit perspective (again, subject to the $30 million floor for any whistleblower subject to a reduction under this provision and the 10 percent statutory minimum referenced above).[277]

At the June 28, 2018 open meeting where this proposal was discussed, two SEC commissioners made public statements in opposition to the proposal to potentially reduce large awards. Commissioner Kara M. Stein stated:

> I am deeply troubled that the proposal would give the Commission authority to depart from its normal analysis for determining the amount of an award in certain circumstances. Currently, to determine the precise award percentage, the Commission considers a list of specific factors, such as the significance of the information provided by the whistleblower. However, under the proposed Rule, the Commission would, in certain circumstances, be able to consider not just the enumerated factors, but also the overall dollar amount of the award. Practically speaking, this means the Commission can reduce the award if, in its sole discretion, it thinks the award is "too large." I am worried that this subjective determination will be used as a means to weaken the Whistleblower Program.[278]

Commissioner Robert J. Jackson, Jr., stated:

> Whistleblowers are crucial to our enforcement efforts, and experts of all stripes have said that this program—which rewards those who make the difficult decision to come forward to help us expose fraud—is among our Staff's most successful endeavors. In addition to certain necessary fixes, the proposal before us today empowers the five of us Commissioners to reduce certain larger whistleblower awards and increase smaller ones.

276. *Id.* at 171.
277. *Id.* at 44.
278. Public Statement of Commissioner Kara M. Stein, Statement on Proposed Amendments to the Commission's Whistleblower Program Rules (June 28, 2018), at https://www.sec.gov/news/public-statement/statement-stein-whistleblower-062818 (last visited Oct. 13, 2018).

Today's proposal risks harming investors by adding two things to this exceptionally successful program that don't belong in the world of whistleblowers: uncertainty and politics. Because I believe that American investors are already dealing with plenty of both, I respectfully dissent.[279]

To date, more than 3,000 comments have been submitted regarding these proposed rule amendments, 1,331 of which are variations of a form letter expressing opposition to the proposed amendment to allow the SEC to reduce awards in the largest cases.[280]

IX.   *Foreign Corrupt Practices Act*

Congress enacted the Foreign Corrupt Practices Act ("FCPA")[281] in order to combat bribery of foreign officials by U.S. companies. The FCPA contains anti-bribery and accounting provisions, and the Department of Justice ("DOJ") and the Securities and Exchange Commission ("SEC") share FCPA enforcement authority. In 2012, the Criminal Division of the DOJ and the Enforcement Division of the SEC issued a *Resource Guide,*[282] which provides comprehensive guidance about their interpretation of the FCPA and approach to enforcement. In the past year, there have been significant developments with respect to (1) the extraterritorial application of the FCPA to foreign individuals who aid and abet or conspire to violate the FCPA's anti-bribery provisions; and (2) the incentives for a company to self-report FCPA violations.

A.   Extraterritorial Application to Accomplices and Conspirators

The FCPA's anti-bribery provisions apply to anyone who falls within one of the following three jurisdictional categories:

---

279. Public Statement of Commissioner Robert J. Jackson, Jr., Statement on Proposed Rules Regarding SEC Whistleblower Program (June 28, 2018), at https://www.sec.gov/news/public-statement/jackson-statement-whistleblowers-062818 (last visited Oct. 13, 2018).

280. Comments on Proposed Rule: Amendments to the Commission's Whistleblower Program Rules (Letter Type A), at https://www.sec.gov/comments/s7-16-18/s71618.htm (last visited Oct. 13, 2018).

281. Pub. L. No. 95-213, §§ 101-104, 91 Stat. 1494 (1977).

282. Criminal Division of the U.S. Department of Justice & Enforcement Division of the U.S. Securities and Exchange Commission, A Resource Guide to the U.S. Foreign Corrupt Practices Act (Nov. 2012) ("Resource Guide"), at https://www.justice.gov/sites/default/files/criminal-fraud/legacy/2015/01/16/guide.pdf (last visited Oct. 1, 2018).

(1) "any issuer which has a class of securities registered pursuant to section 78l of this title [§ 12 of the Exchange Act] or which is required to file reports under section 78o(d) of this title [§ 15(d) of the Exchange Act], or for any officer, director, employee, or agent of such issuer or any stockholder thereof acting on behalf of such issuer;"[283]

(2) "any domestic concern, other than an issuer which is subject to section 78dd-1 of this title, or for any officer, director, employee, or agent of such domestic concern or any stockholder thereof acting on behalf of such domestic concern;"[284] or

(3) "any person other than an issuer that is subject to section 78dd-1 of this title or a domestic concern (as defined in section 78dd-2 of this title), or for any officer, director, employee, or agent of such person or any stockholder thereof acting on behalf of such person, while in the territory of the United States."[285]

Those who aid and abet an FCPA violation are subject to criminal prosecution[286] and civil liability,[287] and those who conspire to violate the FCPA are subject to criminal prosecution.[288]

In the *Resource Guide*, the SEC and the DOJ interpreted the extraterritorial reach of aiding and abetting and conspiracy liability as follows:

A foreign company or individual may be held liable for aiding and abetting an FCPA violation or for conspiring to violate the FCPA, even if the foreign company or individual did not take any act in furtherance of the corrupt payment while in the territory of the United States. In conspiracy cases, the United States generally has jurisdiction over all conspirators where at least one conspirator is an issuer, domestic concern, or commits a reasonably foreseeable overt act within the United States. For example, if a foreign company or individual conspires to violate the FCPA with someone who commits an overt act within the United States, the United States can prosecute the foreign company or individual for conspiracy. The same principle applies to aiding and abetting violations. For instance, even though they took no action in the United States, Japanese and European companies were charged with conspiring with and aiding and abetting a domestic concern's FCPA violations.[289]

In other words, according to the *Resource Guide*, a foreign individual acting outside the U.S. could nonetheless be liable as an accomplice or a

---

283. 15 U.S.C. § 78dd-1(a).
284. 15 U.S.C. § 78dd-2(a); see 15 U.S.C. § 78dd-2(h)(1) (defining "domestic concern").
285. 15 U.S.C. § 78dd-3(a).
286. 18 U.S.C. § 2.
287. 15 U.S.C. § 78t(e).
288. 18 U.S.C. § 371.
289. Resource Guide, at 34 (internal citations omitted).

conspirator, even if he or she was not within the scope of any of the FCPA's three jurisdictional categories.

In a recent case, *United States v. Hoskins*,[290] the Second Circuit disagreed, holding that the "government may not expand the territorial reach of the FCPA by recourse to the conspiracy and complicity statutes."[291] The Second Circuit recognized that, as general principle, "[c]onspiracy and complicity statutes do not cease to apply simply because a statute specifies particular classes of people who violate the law."[292] An exception applies, however, if "Congress demonstrates an affirmative legislative policy to leave some type of participant in a criminal transaction unpunished."[293] After analyzing the text, structure, and legislative history of the FCPA, the Second Circuit concluded that Congress "demonstrated an affirmative legislative policy in the FCPA to limit criminal liability to the enumerated categories of defendants."[294] As an additional rationale for its holding, the Second Circuit applied the presumption against extraterritorial application to reach the same conclusion.[295] Because some of the FCPA's provisions, by their terms, apply extraterritorially, the presumption against extraterritorial application operates to limit that extraterritorial application to those terms.[296]

Notably, even under the Second Circuit's holding, a foreign citizen acting outside of the U.S. is still within the scope of the FCPA's extraterritorial reach—as a primary violator, as an accomplice, or as a conspirator—if he or she qualifies as an "agent" of an issuer[297] or domestic concern.[298] Therefore, it remains to be seen whether the Second Circuit's holding will significantly narrow the reach of the FCPA to foreign citizens. If so, as recognized by Judge Gerard E. Lynch in his concurring opinion, "Congress might want to revisit the statute with this case in mind."[299]

B.   Incentives for Companies to Self-Report FCPA Violations

Companies have historically had incentives to self-report FCPA violations to the SEC and the DOJ, although companies could not be certain that self-reporting violations would affect their liability. One of the factors that the

---

290. United States v. Hoskins, No. 16-100-CR, 2018 WL 4038192 (2d Cir. Aug. 24, 2018).
291. *Id.* at *23.
292. *Id.* at *6.
293. *Id.* at *9.
294. *Id.* at *22.
295. *Id.*
296. *Id.* at *23.
297. 15 U.S.C. § 78dd-1(a).
298. 15 U.S.C. § 78dd-2(a).
299. *Hoskins*, 2018 WL 4038192, at *29 (Lynch, J., concurring).

SEC considers when deciding whether to take enforcement action against a company is whether "the company promptly, completely and effectively disclose[d] the existence of the misconduct to the public, to regulators and to self-regulators."[300] Similarly, one of the factors that the DOJ considers when determining whether to charge a corporation and negotiate plea or other agreements is "the corporation's timely and voluntary disclosure of wrongdoing."[301] Further, under the U.S. Sentencing Guidelines, a company's self-reporting, cooperation, and acceptance of responsibility may decrease the company's culpability score, leading to a reduced fine.[302]

In 2016, the DOJ launched the FCPA Pilot Program, which sought to encourage self-reporting of FCPA violations by providing greater certainty about how self-reporting would affect criminal charges and fines.[303] On November 29, 2017, the DOJ formalized its self-reporting policy, which built on and formalized the FCPA Pilot Program. When announcing the self-reporting policy, Deputy Attorney General Rod Rosenstein explained it as follows:

> In the first year of the Pilot Program, the FCPA Unit received 22 voluntary disclosures, compared to 13 during the previous year. In total, during the year and a half that the Pilot Program was in effect, the FCPA Unit received 30 voluntary disclosures, compared to 18 during the previous 18-month period.
>
> We analyzed the Pilot Program and concluded that it proved to be a step forward in fighting corporate crime. We also determined that there were opportunities for improvement.[304]

The new policy, which is included in the Justice Manual (formerly the United States Attorneys Manual), states as follows:

1. Credit for Voluntary Self-Disclosure, Full Cooperation, and Timely and Appropriate Remediation in FCPA Matters

Due to the unique issues presented in FCPA matters, including their inherently international character and other factors, the FCPA Corporate Enforcement Policy is aimed at providing additional benefits to companies

---

300. Report of Investigation Pursuant to Section 21(a) of the Securities Exchange Act of 1934 and Commission Statement on the Relationship of Cooperation to Agency Enforcement Decisions, SEC Rel. No. 34-44969 (Oct. 23, 2001), at http://www.sec.gov/litigation/investreport/34-44969.htm (last visited Oct. 1, 2018).

301. Justice Manual, § 9-28.300 (Aug. 2008).

302. U.S. Sentencing Guidelines § 8C2.5(g) (2016).

303. Criminal Division of the U.S. Department of Justice, The Fraud Section's Foreign Corrupt Practices Act Enforcement Plan and Guidance (Apr. 5, 2016), at https://www.justice.gov/archives/opa/blog-entry/file/838386/download (last visited Oct. 1, 2018).

304. Deputy Attorney General Rosenstein Delivers Remarks at the 34th International Conference on the Foreign Corrupt Practices Act (Nov. 29, 2017), at https://www.justice.gov/opa/speech/deputy-attorney-general-rosenstein-delivers-remarks-34th-international-conference-foreign (last visited Oct. 1, 2018).

based on their corporate behavior once they learn of misconduct. When a company has voluntarily self-disclosed misconduct in an FCPA matter, fully cooperated, and timely and appropriately remediated, all in accordance with the standards set forth below, there will be a presumption that the company will receive a declination absent aggravating circumstances involving the seriousness of the offense or the nature of the offender. Aggravating circumstances that may warrant a criminal resolution include, but are not limited to, involvement by executive management of the company in the misconduct; a significant profit to the company from the misconduct; pervasiveness of the misconduct within the company; and criminal recidivism.

If a criminal resolution is warranted for a company that has voluntarily self-disclosed, fully cooperated, and timely and appropriately remediated, the Fraud Section:

- will accord, or recommend to a sentencing court, a 50% reduction off of the low end of the U.S. Sentencing Guidelines (U.S.S.G.) fine range, except in the case of a criminal recidivist; and

- generally will not require appointment of a monitor if a company has, at the time of resolution, implemented an effective compliance program.

To qualify for the FCPA Corporate Enforcement Policy, the company is required to pay all disgorgement, forfeiture, and/or restitution resulting from the misconduct at issue.

2. Limited Credit for Full Cooperation and Timely and Appropriate Remediation in FCPA Matters Without Voluntary Self-Disclosure

If a company did not voluntarily disclose its misconduct to the Department of Justice (the Department) in accordance with the standards set forth above, but later fully cooperated and timely and appropriately remediated in accordance with the standards set forth above, the company will receive, or the Department will recommend to a sentencing court, up to a 25% reduction off of the low end of the U.S.S.G. fine range.[305]

The policy also defines "Voluntary Self-Disclosure in FCPA Matters," "Full Cooperation in FCPA Matters," and "Timely and Appropriate Remediation in FCPA Matters."

Of note, the DOJ's self-reporting policy does not protect individuals from prosecution. In addition, the DOJ's self-reporting policy is not binding on the SEC, which may pursue an enforcement action even if the DOJ declines to prosecute.

305. Justice Manual § 9-47.120 (Nov. 2017).

X.   *Regulation of Broker-Dealers and Investment Advisers*

Under current law, investment advisers and broker-dealers are subject to differing standards of conduct. In short, investment advisers are fiduciaries of their clients. As such, investment advisers owe their clients duties of care and loyalty, including the duty to serve the best interests of their clients. Broker-dealers, on the other hand, are generally not fiduciaries, but they do owe their clients a duty of fair dealing. Accordingly, when broker-dealers are making recommendations to their clients, they are required to make recommendations that are suitable to their clients' interests.[306]

Against this backdrop, § 913 of the Dodd-Frank Act required the SEC to conduct a study to evaluate the following:

> (1) the effectiveness of existing legal or regulatory standards of care for brokers, dealers, investment advisers, persons associated with brokers or dealers, and persons associated with investment advisers for providing personalized investment advice and recommendations about securities to retail customers imposed by the Commission and a national securities association, and other Federal and State legal or regulatory standards; and

> (2) whether there are legal or regulatory gaps, shortcomings, or overlaps in legal or regulatory standards in the protection of retail customers relating to the standards of care for brokers, dealers, investment advisers, persons associated with brokers or dealers, and persons associated with investment advisers for providing personalized investment advice about securities to retail customers that should be addressed by rule or statute.[307]

In January 2011, the SEC staff published the report mandated by § 913 of Dodd-Frank. Therein, the staff found that retail investors were confused about the differential standards of conduct applicable to investment advisers and broker-dealers: "[D]espite the extensive regulation of both investment advisers and broker-dealers, retail customers do not understand and are confused by the roles played by investment advisers and broker-dealers, and more importantly, the standards of care applicable to investment advisers and broker-dealers when providing personalized investment advice and recommendations about securities."[308] The SEC staff made the following recommendation:

---

306. *See* SEC Staff, Study on Investment Advisers and Broker-Dealers, at iii-iv (Jan. 2011), at https://www.sec.gov/news/studies/2011/913studyfinal.pdf (last visited Oct. 14, 2018).

307. Dodd-Frank Wall Street Reform and Consumer Protection Act, PL 111-203 § 913(b), July 21, 2010, 124 Stat 1376.

308. SEC Staff, Study on Investment Advisers and Broker-Dealers, at 101 (Jan. 2011), at https://www.sec.gov/news/studies/2011/913studyfinal.pdf (last visited Oct. 14, 2018).

The Commission should engage in rulemaking to implement the uniform fiduciary standard of conduct for broker-dealers and investment advisers when providing personalized investment advice about securities to retail customers. Specifically, the Staff recommends that the uniform fiduciary standard of conduct established by the Commission should provide that:

> the standard of conduct for all brokers, dealers, and investment advisers, when providing personalized investment advice about securities to retail customers (and such other customers as the Commission may be rule provide), shall be to act in the best interest of the customer without regard to the financial or other interest of the broker, dealer, or investment adviser providing the advice.[309]

On April 18, 2018, the SEC proposed (1) a new rule establishing a standard for conduct for broker-dealers; (2) an interpretation of the standard of conduct for investment advisers; and (3) a new disclosure rule applicable to investment advisers and broker-dealers. Although these proposals do not impose as uniform fiduciary standard of conduct, they do seek to bridge the gap between the standards of conduct applicable to broker-dealers and investment advisers.

First, with respect to broker-dealers, the SEC proposed a new Regulation Best Interest.[310] Under the proposal, a broker-dealer making a recommendation to a retail customer would be required "to act in the best interest of the retail customer at the time the recommendation is made without placing the financial or other interest of the broker, dealer, or natural person who is an associated person of a broker or dealer making the recommendation ahead of the interest of the retail customer."[311] This best interest obligation would include three specific components: a Disclosure Obligation, a Care Obligation, and Conflict of Interest Obligations:

- The broker, dealer or natural person who is an associated person of a broker or dealer, prior to or at the time of the recommendation, reasonably discloses to the retail customer, in writing, the material facts relating to the scope and terms of the relationship with the retail customer and all material conflicts of interest that are associated with the recommendation (the "Disclosure Obligation");

- The broker, dealer or natural person who is an associated person of a broker or dealer, in making the recommendation, exercises reasonable diligence, care, skill, and prudence to: (1) understand the potential risks and rewards associated with the recommendation, and have a reasonable basis to believe that the recommendation could be in the best interest of at least some retail customers; (2) have a reasonable basis to

---

309. *Id.* at 109-10.
310. Regulation Best Interest, SEC Release No. 83062 (Apr. 18, 2018).
311. *Id.* at 44.

believe that the recommendation is in the best interest of a particular retail customer based on the retail customer's investment profile and the potential risks and rewards associated with the recommendation; and (3) have a reasonable basis to believe that a series of recommended transactions, even if in the retail customer's best interest when viewed in isolation, is not excessive and is in the retail customer's best interest when taken together in light of the retail customer's investment profile (herein, "Care Obligation");

- The broker or dealer establishes, maintains, and enforces written policies and procedures reasonably designed to identify and at a minimum disclose, or eliminate, all material conflicts of interest that are associated with recommendations; and

- The broker or dealer establishes, maintains, and enforces written policies and procedures reasonably designed to identify and disclose and mitigate, or eliminate, material conflicts of interest arising from financial incentives associated with such recommendations (the last two together, the "Conflict of Interest Obligations").[312]

Second, with respect to investment advisers, the SEC issued a proposed interpretation of the standards of conduct for investment advisers in order to "reaffirm—and in some cases clarify—certain aspects of the fiduciary duty that an investment adviser owes to its clients."[313] In the proposed interpretation, the SEC noted that "[a]n investment adviser's fiduciary duty is similar to, but not the same as, the proposed obligations of broker-dealers under Regulation Best Interest."[314] The proposed interpretation provides guidance on the following aspects of the duty of care: "(i) the duty to act and to provide advice that is in the best interest of the client; (ii) the duty to seek best execution of a client's transactions where the adviser has the responsibility to select broker-dealers to execute client trades; and (iii) the duty to provide advice and monitoring over the course of the relationship."[315] In addition, the proposed interpretation provides guidance on the following aspects of the duty of loyalty: (i) "an adviser must make full and fair disclosure to its clients of all material facts relating to the advisory relationship";[316] and (ii) "an adviser must seek to avoid conflicts of interest with its clients, and, at a minimum make full and fair disclosure of all material conflicts of interest that could affect the advisory relationship."[317]

---

312. *Id.* at 44-45.
313. Proposed Commission Interpretation Regarding Standard of Conduct for Investment Advisers; Request for Comment on Enhancing Investment Adviser Regulation, SEC Release No. IA-4889, at 5 (Apr. 18, 2018).
314. *Id.*
315. *Id.* at 9.
316. *Id.* at 15.
317. *Id.* at 15-16.

There is not much daylight between the proposed "best interest" standard for broker-dealers and the proposed interpretive guidance on the standards of conduct for investment advisers. Commissioner Hester M. Peirce provided the following preliminary analysis:

> In comparing the proposed Regulation Best Interest standard as well as a broker-dealer's other requirements under the securities laws to an adviser's fiduciary duty as described in the proposed interpretive release, only two differences stand out. First, an adviser generally has an ongoing duty to monitor over the course of its relationship with its client, while a broker-dealer generally does not. Second, a broker-dealer must either mitigate or eliminate any material financial conflict of interest it may have with its client. An adviser is required only to disclose such a conflict. Rhetoric aside, arguably proposed Regulation Best Interest would subject broker-dealers to an even more stringent standard than the fiduciary standard outlined in the Commission's proposed interpretation.[318]

Accordingly, she forecast that, if these proposals are adopted, more broker-dealers may elect to convert to investment advisers, which could lead to fewer options for investors to obtain investment advice outside the context of fee-based accounts.[319]

In addition to the aforementioned Regulation Best Interest and interpretive guidance, the SEC proposed a new disclosure rule, pursuant to which both broker-dealers and investment advisers must provide clients a "customer or client relationship summary" (on a new Form CRS):

> We are proposing to require registered investment advisers and registered broker-dealers to deliver a relationship summary to retail investors. In the case of an investment adviser, initial delivery would occur before or at the time the firm enters into an investment advisory agreement with the retail investor; in the case of a broker-dealer, initial delivery would occur before or at the time the retail investor first engages the firm's services. Dual registrants would deliver the relationship summary at the earlier of entering into an investment advisory agreement with the retail investor or the retail investor engaging the firm's services.

> The relationship summary would be as short as practicable (limited to four pages or equivalent limit if in electronic format), with a mix of tabular and narrative information, and contain sections covering: (i) introduction; (ii) the relationships and services the firm offers to retail investors; (iii) the

---

318. Commissioner Hester M. Peirce, Speech, What's in a Name? Regulation Best Interest v. Fiduciary (July 24, 2018), at https://www.sec.gov/news/speech/speech-peirce-072418 (last visited Oct. 14, 2018).

319. *Id.* ("Although we tried to be cognizant of these access concerns, given the relative balance of the two standards, I fear that more and more broker-dealers will decide to become advisers that offer only fee-based accounts resulting in many Americans being shut out from receiving any investment advice.").

standard of conduct applicable to those services; (iv) the fees and costs that retail investors will pay; (v) comparisons of brokerage and investment advisory services (for standalone broker-dealers and investment advisers); (vi) conflicts of interest; (vii) where to find additional information, including whether the firm and its financial professionals currently have reportable legal or disciplinary events and who to contact about complaints; and (viii) key questions for retail investors to ask the firm's financial professional.[320]

As commentators have noted, "[t]he SEC did not address how a dual-hatted individual who is associated with a broker-dealer and investment adviser that are not affiliated could comply with the Proposed Disclosure Rules in a way that would not be confusing to clients or potential clients."[321]

Finally, on March 15, 2018, the Fifth Circuit held that the Department of Labor ("DOL") lacked statutory authority to promulgate its so-called Fiduciary Rule and thus vacated the rule in its entirety.[322] In short, the Fiduciary Rule would have defined "persons who provide investment advice or recommendations for a fee or other compensation with respect to assets of a plan or IRA as fiduciaries in a wider array of advice relationships."[323] The Fiduciary Rule was promulgated under the administration of President Obama, and President Trump had already directed the DOL to reexamine the rule.[324] In the wake of the Fifth Circuit's decision, the DOL has indicated that it will not be enforcing the Fiduciary Rule.[325]

XI.   Proxy Advisory Firms and Shareholder Proposals

On July 30, 2018, SEC Chairman Jay Clayton announced an upcoming SEC staff roundtable on the proxy process.[326] Therein, he proposed potential

---

320. Proposed Rule, Form CRS Relationship Summary; Amendments to Form ADV; Required Disclosures in Retail Communications and Restrictions on the Use of Certain Names or Titles, SEC Release No. 34-83063, at 13-14 (Apr. 18, 2018).

321. Dechert LLP, SEC Proposes Best Interest Standard for Broker-Dealers, Related Investment Adviser Guidance and New Customer Relationship Summary Form, at 18 (July 2018), at https://www.dechert.com/content/dam/dechert%20files/onpoint/2018/7/OnPoint%20-%20SEC%20Proposes%20Best%20Interest%20Standard%20for%20Broker-Dealers%20-%20July%202018.pdf (last visited Oct. 14, 2018).

322. Chamber of Commerce v. Department of Labor, 885 F.3d 360 (2018).

323. Definition of the Term "Fiduciary"; Conflict of Interest Rule — Retirement Investment Advice, 81 Fed. Reg. 20946-01 (April 8, 2016).

324. Presidential Memorandum on Fiduciary Duty Rule (Feb. 3, 2017), at https://www.whitehouse.gov/presidential-actions/presidential-memorandum-fiduciary-duty-rule/ (last visited Oct. 14, 2018).

325. Carmen Castro-Pagan & Madison Alder, *Labor Dept. Won't Enforce the Obama-Era Fiduciary Rule*, BLOOMBERG NEWS (March 16, 2018), at https://www.bna.com/labor-dept-wont-n57982089974/ (last visited Oct. 14, 2018).

326. SEC Chairman Jay Clayton, Public Statement, Statement Announcing SEC Staff Roundtable on the Proxy Process (July 30, 2018), at https://www.sec.gov/news/public-statement/statement-announcing-sec-staff-roundtable-proxy-process (Oct. 14, 2018).

agenda items that could significantly affect proxy advisory firms and shareholder proposals.

A. Proxy Advisory Firms

First, Chairman Clayton previewed a potential discussion about the role and regulation of proxy advisory firms:

> Proxy advisory firms provide a number of services related to proxy voting, which include aggregating and standardizing information, providing platforms for managing votes, and providing voting recommendations. Areas that may warrant particular attention include:
>
> - Whether various factors, including legal requirements, have resulted in investment advisers to funds and other clients relying on proxy advisory firms for information aggregation and voting recommendations to a greater extent than they should, and whether the extent of reliance on these firms is in the best interests of investment advisers and their clients, including funds and fund shareholders.
>
> - Whether issuers are being given an appropriate opportunity to raise concerns if they disagree with a proxy advisory firm's recommendations, including, in particular, if the recommendation is based on erroneous, materially incomplete, or outdated information.
>
> - Whether there is sufficient transparency about a proxy advisory firm's voting policies and procedures so that companies, investors, and other market participants can understand how the advisory firm reached its voting recommendations on a particular matter, and whether comparisons of recommendations across similarly situated companies have value.
>
> - Whether there are conflicts of interest, including with respect to related consulting services provided by proxy advisory firms, and, if so, whether those conflicts are adequately disclosed and mitigated.
>
> - The appropriate regulatory regime for proxy advisory firms and whether prior staff guidance about investment advisers' responsibilities in voting client proxies and retaining proxy advisory firms should be modified, rescinded, or supplemented.

Then, on September 13, 2018, the staff of the Division of Investment Management issued a statement withdrawing two no-action letters related to proxy advisory firms:

> In developing the agenda for the roundtable, the staff has been considering (among other topics) whether prior staff guidance about investment

advisers' responsibilities in voting client proxies and retaining proxy advisory firms should be modified, rescinded or supplemented. Staff guidance is non-binding and does not create enforceable legal rights or obligations.

With this pending Roundtable and other policy considerations in mind, the staff of the Division of Investment Management has recently re-examined the letters that the staff issued in 2004 to Egan-Jones Proxy Services (May 27, 2004) and Institutional Shareholder Services, Inc. (Sept. 15, 2004). Taking into account developments since 2004, the staff has determined to withdraw these letters, effective today. The staff is providing this notice of withdrawal of the letters in order to facilitate the discussion at the Roundtable and looks forward to receiving information and feedback from stakeholders with multiple perspectives at the Roundtable, including on the staff guidance in Staff Legal Bulletin No. 20 (June 30, 2014). The staff expects to utilize what it learns in any future recommendations to the Commission with respect to proxy advisory firms.[327]

One commentator explained the implication of the withdrawal of these two no-action letters as follows:

To satisfy their fiduciary duty to clients, investment advisers generally must adopt and implement policies and procedures reasonably designed to ensure that the adviser votes proxies in the best interests of its clients. The two letters that the SEC now has withdrawn stated that one way an adviser could demonstrate that it had voted the proxies in the clients' best interests was to vote such proxies according to the recommendations of an independent third party. Thus, many investment advisers took advantage of this guidance and relied on the recommendations of one of the well-established proxy advisory firms. Apparently, investment advisers can no longer rely on the recommendation of a proxy advisory firm, without more.[328]

In response to the staff's decision, SEC Commissioner Robert J. Jackson Jr. expressed concern "that our efforts to fix corporate democracy will be stymied by misguided and controversial efforts to regulate proxy advisors—the firms that advise American shareholder how to vote in corporate elections."[329]

---

327. SEC Division of Investment Management, Public Statement, Statement Regarding Staff Proxy Advisory Letters (Sept. 13, 2018), at https://www.sec.gov/news/public-statement/statement-regarding-staff-proxy-advisory-letters (last visited Oct. 14, 2018).

328. Michael S. Melbinger, Winston & Strawn LLP, *SEC Withdraws Support for Proxy Advisory Firms*, EXECUTIVE COMPENSATION BLOG (Oct. 8, 2018), at https://www.winston.com/en/executive-compensation-blog/sec-withdraws-support-for-proxy-advisory-firms.html (last visited Oct. 14, 2018).

329. Commissioner Robert J. Jackson Jr., Statement on Shareholder Voting (Sept. 14, 2018), at https://www.sec.gov/news/public-statement/statement-jackson-091418#_ftnref1 (last visited Oct. 14, 2018).

B. Shareholder Proposals

Under current Rule 14a-8, a shareholder can submit a shareholder proposal by satisfying the following threshold requirement: "[Y]ou must have continuously held at least $2,000 in market value, or 1%, of the company's securities entitled to be votes on the proposal at the meeting for at least one year by the date you submit the proposal."[330]

As announced by Chairman Clayton, a second potential topic for discussion at the upcoming SEC staff roundtable on the proxy process is shareholder proposals:

> The shareholder proposal process is a channel for shareholders to engage with the U.S. public companies in which they invest on specific topics. All shareholders, as the ultimate owners of the company, bear the costs associated with management's consideration of a proposal and its inclusion in the proxy statement. And, those same shareholders may benefit from the engagement and potential for enhanced performance brought about by consideration of a shareholder proposal. Many market participants believe this dynamic has enhanced company performance. Many market participants also believe that the costs of this process could be significantly reduced without limiting (and potentially increasing) the benefits of shareholder engagement. In this vein, it often is noted that a small group of shareholders submits a significant percentage of the total number of shareholder proposals each year.

Areas of the shareholder engagement process that may warrant particular attention include:

- Whether the current thresholds for minimum ownership (e.g., shares held and length of time) to submit a proposal to be included in the company's proxy statement appropriately consider the interests of all shareholders, taking into account the potential benefits to shareholders of a proposal (or resubmission) being considered or adopted, as well as the costs associated with the inclusion of a proposal (or resubmission) in the proxy statement.

- Further, whether rules that allow companies to omit resubmitted proposals that received less than 3%, 6%, or 10% of the vote, depending on how many times the subject matter has been voted on in the last five years, are appropriate.

- Whether meaningful ownership in the company can be demonstrated by factors other than the amount invested and the length of time shares are held.

---

330. 17 C.F.R. § 240.14a-8(b)(1).

- Whether the voices of long-term retail investors (who invest directly and indirectly through mutual funds, ETFs, and other products) are appropriately represented in the shareholder proposal process and in the shareholder engagement dynamic more generally.[331]

Among those who view shareholder proposals as a nuisance that empowers activist shareholders, there is significant support for raising the minimum ownership threshold to submit a shareholder proposal. For example, in a recent Department of the Treasury report to President Trump, the Treasury made the following recommendation:

Treasury recommends that the $2,000 holding requirement, which was instituted 30 years ago, be substantially revised. The SEC might also want to explore options that better align shareholder interests (such as considering the shareholder's dollar holding in company stock as a percentage of his or her net liquid assets) when evaluating eligibility, rather than basing eligibility solely on a fixed dollar holding in stock or percentage of the company's outstanding stock.[332]

Likewise, in 2017, the U.S. House of Representatives passed the Financial CHOICE Act, which would have significantly raised the threshold for submitting shareholder proposals as follows:

(1) eliminate the option to satisfy the holding requirement by holding a certain dollar amount;

(2) require the shareholder to hold 1 percent of the issuer's securities entitled to be voted on the proposal, or such greater percentage as determined by the Commission; and

(3) adjust the 1 year holding period to 3 years.[333]

The elimination of the dollar amount threshold without a substantial decrease in the percentage ownership threshold would effectively foreclose shareholder proposals to most investors. For this reason, Professor David Webber has criticized the CHOICE Act's approach, arguing that it would

---

331. SEC Chairman Jay Clayton, Public Statement, Statement Announcing SEC Staff Roundtable on the Proxy Process (July 30, 2018), at https://www.sec.gov/news/public-statement/statement-announcing-sec-staff-roundtable-proxy-process (Oct. 14, 2018).

332. U.S. Department of the Treasury, A Financial System That Creates Economic Opportunities: Capital Markets, at 32 (Oct. 2017), at https://www.treasury.gov/press-center/press-releases/Documents/A-Financial-System-Capital-Markets-FINAL-FINAL.pdf (last visited Oct. 14, 2018).

333. H.R. 10 § 844(b) (passed the House on June 8, 2017) (received by the Senate on June 12, 2017).

"reduce stockholders' ability to shape the companies they own and hold corporate managers accountable."[334]

XII.   *Conclusion*

This is a dynamic time for securities law, and it will be fascinating to see what the next year holds. The author welcomes feedback on the coverage in this year's *Updates in Securities Regulation* as well as recommendations of topics for inclusion in potential future editions.

---

334. David H. Webber, *Big Corporations Are Trying to Silence Their Own Shareholders*, WASH. POST (Apr. 13, 2017), at https://www.washingtonpost.com/opinions/voter-suppression-corporate-style/2017/04/13/bbe62880-1ed5-11e7-be2a-3a1fb24d4671_story.html?utm_term=.ef9bf6f75b01 (last visited Oct. 14, 2018).

www.ingramcontent.com/pod-product-compliance
Lightning Source LLC
Chambersburg PA
CBHW061838220326
41599CB00027B/5326